# A Sparge Bag on the Washing Line

*A diary*

# Julia Thorley

First published in 2019 in the UK

3P Publishing
C E C, London Road
Corby
NN17 5EU

A catalogue number for this book is available from
the British Library

ISBN 978-1-911559-91-7

Cover design: Marie-Louise O'Neill

Additional illustrations: Gill Arthey

*For Clive, without whom...*

## MAY

## 31 May

On the eve of Clive's retirement, a friend tells me that when her brother retired her sister-in-law took a lease on a shop and started a women's fashion business so they wouldn't both be in the house all day.

Clive has been saying for a while that his feelings about the Big Day have swung from fear to elation, to worry, to relief, to bewilderment and all points in between. Of course, it's going to be strange for me, too. We have joked about him getting under my feet, but actually it's not that funny. I work from home, so he will be here, in my space, denting my routine.

We have agreed we shan't row about our new circumstances for a month and then we will vent. I know I'm bossy, but I shall try not to suggest that he could do this or that to fill his days. He knows he can be lazy and has agreed to try to resist the urge to sit and play Hearthstone on his laptop, at least not all day, every day. We'll see.

So tonight we kick off the rest of our lives with takeaway pizza with the 'boys', that is, grown-up sons Sam and Joe, and Joe's girlfriend Caitlin who, as always, arrives with an appropriate balloon in hand to get the party started. Much chatter and laughter ensues.

# JUNE

## 1 June

We have arranged a weekend away in Tenby to walk a stretch of the Pembrokeshire coastal path. The journey does not go well. We have our usual 'conversation' about the merits of satnav (him) versus maps and road signs (me). The traffic is heavy and by the time we take our planned break in Ross-on-Wye I'm in full-on toddler mode and spoiling for a fight. We stop for a sandwich, which we eat leaning up against the open boot of the car. When a passer-by stops and stares, I snarl at him: 'Know me again, would you?' He is clearly taken aback by what I now admit was my unnecessary venom and seems rooted to the tarmac. I look away, petulant and possibly a little ashamed of myself.

We find an independent coffee shop, where I am further enraged when a woman brings a hideous pug inside. That's bad enough, but then she picks it up and kisses it, before perching it on her lap so its mouth and balls are at table – and therefore food – height. I bite my tongue.

We do eventually make it to Tenby, of course, and the Strathmore B&B is charming. There is another slight wobble when we set off in search of dinner and find the town is full of families with squawking children and gaggles of hefty, underdressed girls out on the lash, but we eventually settle on fish and chips and, thankfully, disaster is averted.

Meanwhile in the real world, the Visa network is experiencing what it calls 'technical difficulties' that mean no one can pay for anything with plastic. The next day, the news is awash with stories of shopkeepers rummaging in the back of the stockroom to retrieve old-fashioned card machines and people having to leave their names and addresses with petrol stations. Some had to leave their children as collateral while they dashed home to search for cash down the back of the sofa. OK, maybe not that, but you'd have thought the world had ended, rather than suffered a bit of a blip for a couple of hours. The conspiracy theorists were in their element.

## 2 June

After a fabulous night's sleep, we wake to blue skies and twinkling seas. We have planned to walk a stretch of the coast path up to Saundersfoot, which looks doable. This turns out to be more strenuous than we had anticipated (note to self: check the contour lines), but after a cuppa and a potter on the beach, we decide we are not yet of an age to ride the bus back and make it on foot, to be revived by a welcome pint of Reverend James.

Idle chat inevitably turns to work. Clive slips into a lengthy chunter about paperwork he'd been involved with last week and refers to his former colleagues as 'we' until I point out it is now 'they'.

## 3 June

We return home via Colby Woodland Garden, a National Trust property. (We are so middle class.) Even this early in the season, the teashop is busy and the outside tables are filling up nicely, especially those with a parasol over them. Sensing that a passing couple are seeking shade, I invite them to share our table, as we will be leaving soon anyway. The woman gives me a tight-lipped smile and makes a sort of whimpering noise. They turn and go off to place an order, but don't return. I imagine they think we look a bit dodgy and have taken sanctuary inside. Perhaps they think I'm going to ask them for money.

Back at home, we struggle in with our bags and step over a pile of leaflets offering all manner of unwanted services, together with a few bits of post. Amongst them is a letter written from me to me. To explain: one of the familiar activities in writing groups is to get participants to write a letter to themselves, which the group leader will post at some unspecified date, and this is one such letter. I have written: 'Retirement for Clive will mean changes for everyone and some will be hard to swallow. Reserve judgement. Just because you will be affected by a decision doesn't mean you have a right to take part in the process of making it. Bide your time.'

## 4 June

Monday morning and I kick off my day as I do most mornings with a video from 'Yoga With Adriene', my go-to girl for online classes. Today's recommendation from YouTube is 'Gentle Yoga For Seniors'. How does it know?

I'm beavering away in my home office when Clive comes in dressed for the allotment, which I take as a good sign. He checks his phone and laughs: 'My calendar says I'm on the early shift this week. I don't think so!' He sets off, saying something about planting courgettes and I return to my screen. He comes back several hours later, muttering darkly about slugs.

## 5 June

When my mother-in-law died at the age of 97, we discovered that she had kept pretty much every bill and receipt that had ever come her way. I'd always known that she had a strong distrust of financial institutions and kept meticulous records, but we hadn't been expecting to find decades' worth of yellowing paper secured on a metal meat skewer in the pantry. This does explain, however, why Clive is so obsessive about our own financial records. He is king of the spreadsheet and checks the bank online every day. In the run-up to retirement, he monitored his pension plan in painstaking detail, which made me grateful and irritated in equal measure.

One of the things we found in Flora's paperwork was a share certificate from Lloyds Banking Group. Her becoming a shareholder must have happened by default following some flotation or other, because I can't imagine for a moment that she would have done it deliberately. This legacy is now in Clive's hands (he is an only child) and the latest statement, which arrives today, brings news of a dividend payable of £2.71. Is that sufficient to buy a celebratory pint?

**6 June**
Clive says, 'It just feels like I'm on holiday at the moment,' followed moments later by, 'Oh heck. What have I done?'

**7 June**
My old bass guitar is dusted off and I nurse Clive through the rigours of the 'good bit' of Fleetwood

Mac's 'The Chain' and the basic theory behind 12-bar blues. Oh dear.

## 8 June

We have lunch with our old friend Debs today. She is newly 60 (surely not!) and she and Clive spend some time comparing notes of what freebies you can get at this milestone age. While you can't get your state pension until the date the government has decreed, you can get some stuff once you hit 60. Debs knows about these things and is already getting her money's worth out of her Senior Railcard. Then there's free eye tests, free prescriptions, the B&Q Diamond Club Card, discounts on insurance, cheaper English Heritage and National Trust membership, ad hoc discounts for entrance to theatres, two-for-one deals in pubs, Silver Screening at the Odeon: is there no end to the bounty?

## 9 and 10 June

Clive is away for the weekend at an USDAW conference. Notwithstanding that he's no longer working, he still supports the aims of the union and is keen to attend as a lay member. Nothing to do with all the food and beer, I'm sure. I have two days to myself.

## 11 June

Little bit of a tetchy day and Clive hovers around rather more than I would have liked. Also, is it wrong that I'm mildly irritated by his new habit of not returning the toothpaste to the appropriate place in the bathroom? Maybe he's always done this and I'm only just noticing. It probably won't matter tomorrow.

**12 June**
'I dreamt about work last night,' Clive says, before I've even got my eyes open. I fight back the words, 'You mean where you used to work.'

He continues, 'I was back on site and a chap I used to work with somewhere else was there. Then other people started to appear and I didn't know any of them, but this other bloke did. Weird.'

Other people's dreams are always boring, but you feel obliged to comment on them. The best I can manage this early in the day is, 'Well, you don't have to be a psychologist to work that one out.' There is a harrumph.

This afternoon Clive comes in very useful, though. I am planning a presence on a stall with Northants Authors and need a massive photocopying and stapling job doing. I am grateful for his help and at the end of the afternoon he presents me with 35 copies of a short story project I've written called *The Harmonium's Last Chord*. I probably won't sell any – not even at £1 a pop – but you never know. (Postscript: I sell one copy, and two copies of my short story collection, *Nine Lives*.)

## 13 June

Clive is definitely in a funny mood this morning. He's quiet, which makes me worry that he's thinking about something.

After denying several times that there's anything wrong, eventually he says, 'It's nothing, really. I've just realised that this is my life now. You're still busy, rushing around doing stuff and at 10 o'clock I was still in my dressing-gown playing bingo on my phone.'

All of this is undoubtedly true, but I just say, 'Oh well,' which probably isn't much help. Before he'd even come downstairs, I had washed up last night's pots, done a half-hour yoga practice, tidied round a bit and had my breakfast.

When I start to put in a load of washing, Clive says, 'I could have done that.'

Yes, I think, you could.

In due course, he bundles some seed packets and a trowel into his rucksack and goes off to the allotment. I expect he'll be there all day now. Meanwhile, I have two yoga classes to teach and a stack of editing to get through before dance rehearsals tonight.

It seems rather soon for the novelty of freedom to have worn off. If it were me who had been released from the shackles, I would have so much I wanted to do: books to read, chains of thought to follow, places to visit, friends to contact, cupboards to sort out. I guess we're just very different.

**14 June**

One of Clive's best friends has had a health scare. The good news is he doesn't have prostate cancer, but it was a worrying time and gave us both pause for thought. What struck me most, though, was that this friend hadn't said anything to Clive, just that he was 'on the sick' and would be in touch in a couple of days' time. If one of my girlfriends hadn't told me she was going through something this grim I'd be a bit put out. Well, it just wouldn't happen.

Elsewhere, the football World Cup starts today (deep joy). There aren't many posters up in windows or silly flags festooning builders' vans this time around. Could it be that we are finally accepting that 1966 was a fluke and we – by which I mean England – haven't come anywhere close since, notwithstanding Italia '90 and Gazza's tears?

**15 June**

Clive puts his free time to good use today by baking. I'm quite partial to a cereal bar. Yes, I know they're loaded with sugar and ridiculously expensive, but they are very tasty and so convenient. Anyway, Clive has studied the ingredients list on a package of Special K Blackcurrant and Pumpkin Seed Protein Bars and devised his own version. The results are excellent. I shall let him stay a bit longer.

## 16 June

I've been booked to do a talk at Towcester Library, a kind of 'meet the author' event. Clive says he'll come with me to be my roadie and generally be supportive. When we arrive, we are greeted by a very apologetic member of staff, who'd booked me, saying the regular crew who go to every event every month wouldn't be there and she wasn't expecting many folk. I am a bit disappointed, but also quite relieved, as I'm quite nervous. In the event there is an audience of ten. I sell four books and leave behind another six to go in the library's local author section.

Clive is no doubt anxious to accrue some Brownie points ahead of the evening, because he is off out with his former workmates for his leaving do. Yes, this is a fortnight after his last day, but there were various logistics reasons for this. At the appointed hour I take him over to The Saxon Crown in Corby. 'The lads' are going to fund a taxi home for him, because I flatly refuse to fetch him back: not after the last time…

We have already decided we will bypass the row and go straight to him sleeping in the spare room tonight.

## 17 June

Last night's sleeping arrangements worked well and Clive enjoys a bit of a lie-in without any tutting and sighing from me. I'm being unfair, actually. He seems to have behaved with the decorum that might be expected of a retired gentleman. At least, if he feels rough he doesn't show it. On rising, he says he'd 'done it justice' but hadn't let himself down. I had wondered if it might unsettle him to see his former colleagues, but he declared himself 'well out of it'.

It's Father's Day, so Sam, Joe and Caitlin come over with gifts and cards. We order a takeaway, which we eat while watching *Dead Pool* on Caitlin's recommendation. Both food and film are surprisingly good.

## 18 June

An uneventful day, marked only by the quest to find some huge metal saucepans, and by huge I mean at least 10-litre capacity. For some time now Clive has been brewing beer from kits and I have to say it's rather tasty, but the process is messy and seems to require more and more space with each batch. Now he's decided that, not content with swilling out the kitchen at regular intervals in the quest for the perfect pint, he wants to explore all-grain brewing, which basically means buying all the components separately for what is called a SMaSH brew (single malt and single hop). He has found a 'simple' recipe online, which has necessitated buying something called Maris Otter, which is not the pseudonym of a Victorian novelist, but a variety of barley.

Ian Bosworth, who runs Copper Kettle Homebrewing and is the fount of all knowledge on such matters, has recommended two big pans, a potato masher and an expanse of muslin as prerequisite for this latest adventure. He also sells Clive something called a sparge bag, which is used to rinse the grains. I can't believe that sparge is a real word, but there it is in *Chambers*. It comes from the Latin word spargere, which means to sprinkle. (You're welcome.)

A trawl of eBay and Freecycle comes to nothing, so Clive decides to buy new and orders a set of four pans, the biggest of which will hold 20 US quarts, which is as near as dammit 19 litres. One of the benefits of home-brewed beer is its low per-pint cost. I fear that the purchase of all this extra equipment, which may well only be used once, might negate this element.

## 19 June

The wheels of commerce turn slowly, so it is only this morning that Clive receives his final payslip for £666.51. You'd have thought they could have rounded it up. Even so, it's a line drawn under that chapter.

## 20 June

While Clive busies himself with some high-grade cleaning ahead of a visit by my family on Sunday, I go about my usual frantic Wednesday routine.

Today's session of teaching yoga at the gym is particularly challenging. I arrive to find the car park full to bursting, due to what I later learn is a gathering of podiatrists in the next-door conference centre. I am barely through the door before I am accosted by a student, justifiably complaining that the online booking system is still showing classes are full when they're not, and the air conditioning isn't working. It is a sticky start in many ways.

Because the room is so hot, we agree to keep the doors ajar. One opens on to the corridor leading to the changing rooms and the swimming pool, so there is a constant stream of folk going past our session. Many are talking loudly into their phones and quite a few stop to gawp at us as we pose with our tails in the air. The other door opens on to a reception area, where people are chatting and clinking coffee cups against a background of loud music. We acknowledge the distraction, but try to keep our focus inwards, like good yogis. I smile on the outside. Highlight of the session comes when we are moving into Eagle posture, just as Lynyrd Skynyrd's 'Freebird' comes on.

I relay all this in an excitable blurt when I get home, barely pausing for breath. Then I continue with my day: editing and writing, teaching a second class, then trying to be in two places at once in the evening – an authors' get-together and a dance rehearsal – and almost succeeding.

That evening, when I finally collapse in front of the TV with a sandwich of cream-cheese and crisps, Clive suggests that perhaps I am doing too much. It occurs to me that my tornado-like progress through the house might already be starting to get on his nerves. I shall need to watch this.

## 21 June

In the continuing blitz of the kitchen before the arrival of The Family on Sunday, I find Clive hoovering the back of the fridge. I don't know whether to laugh or cry. We are expecting my mum, my brother Neil, his wife Melanie and their son Matthew, and other brother Tim, his wife Anne and their children Freddie and Rebecca: quite a lot for our small house.

## 22 June

There is a touch of stress in the air today. I am mithered about preparations for Sunday and aware that I am going to be out all day tomorrow. My computer has slowed down virtually to a standstill and by six o'clock I am ready to blow – and blow I do. It is unfortunate for Clive that this comes just at the moment he's chosen to treat himself to half an hour on the PS3. It was probably unfair to spit out, 'You're not on holiday, you know!' After all, he has done quite a lot of cleaning and cooking and general preparation.

He knows me well enough after all these years not to fight back. The best thing to do when I'm having one of these meltdowns is to stand well out of the way and let me get on with it. I don't believe in astrology, but if I did I'd say I exhibit typical Scorpio behaviour in that I lash out without warning, but then calm down again just as quickly.

I apologise later and all is well. I don't deserve him.

## 23 June

Today we have a much-needed day apart. I go to Stanwick Lakes to take part in the Raunds Ukulele Orchestra's all-day extravaganza. Clive spends the day cooking, which he loves and I hate. Hence, a good result all round.

## 24 June

Well, all Clive's hard work pays off and we entertain my family in good style. It is the first time Caitlin has met most of them, but she launches in bravely and immediately endears herself to my mother by (a) greeting her with a hug and (b) having long curly hair. Mum does love long curly hair. She (Caitlin) and Joe stick it out until nearly six o'clock, which shows great fortitude. Sam 'bounces', as he puts it, when the majority of the male contingent decamps into the house to watch the football (England 6, Panama 1), so he decides he might as well go home. I send him on his way with a hug and a small food parcel.

## 25 June

It seems we are to have a heatwave. Certainly today it is gloriously warm. Clive disappears to the allotment and comes back with the world's smallest courgettes, some strawberries and several pounds of blackcurrants. And so it begins.

## 26 June

A rather mopey Clive today declares it is too hot to go to the allotment, so he sets about turning fruit into wine. I can only hope that the results will be worth all the stickiness.

While sitting in the garden topping and tailing, he has a chat with our neighbour over the fence. He retired a couple of years ago and tells Clive it was a decision he's never regretted. Apparently, joining a gym has been a revelation and he encourages Clive to do the same. I shall not hold my breath.

There is also a round of golf in the early evening, with long-time pal Paul. Plans for the usual lads' weekend away have been thrown into chaos due to various weddings and work commitments, but it looks as though they have finally settled on a date and a vague destination. I can't help feeling that if they actually picked up the phone and spoke to one another, rather than trying to communicate via text, firm plans would be made with greater efficiency.

## 27 June

There is more brewing activity today, but the highpoint comes in the afternoon when Germany are knocked out of the World Cup after losing 2-0 to South Korea. This is only the second time they have gone home at the group stage, the last being in 1938. Anyone know the German for 'You're not singing any more!'?

## 28 June

There is a blip of excitement this morning when it looks as though the first chunk of pension money is on its way. In the event, it transpires that although it has left the fund (I don't really understand these things), it hasn't actually landed in our bank account, being held somewhere in the twilight of the BACS system. The champagne is put back on ice.

There is little sign of activity today as Clive is in limbo, waiting for the England match this evening. It turns out not to be worth the wait – England 1, Belgium 2 – but since both teams were already through, neither tried especially hard to win. The match was academic, and could easily have been decided by the toss of a coin. I feel sorry for the fans who schlepped all the way to the Kaliningrad Stadium to be treated with such disdain.

## 29 June

Clive is in the midst of an ongoing wrangle with Virgin about mobile phone contracts (don't ask). He rings them again this morning to try and get it resolved, which seems to involve him, saying 'No, no, *no*, you're not listening,' several times with undertones of increasing exasperation.

I watch from a safe distance as he slowly turns into Victor Meldrew and, not for the first time, I wrap myself in the smugness that can only be enjoyed by someone who has a PAYG phone that costs a fiver a month. When the little boy who sold me my car last year saw it, he accused me of being a drug-dealer. Apparently my phone looks like a 'burner', a cheap phone that is used temporarily and then thrown away. Think *Breaking Bad*.

Business concluded to his partial satisfaction, Clive goes out into the garden to vent his frustration with hammer and nail by reroofing the shed. It's a man thing.

## 30 June

Clive is doing battle with a blackbird that has taken a fancy to his blackcurrants. Notwithstanding a sophisticated defence strategy that has necessitated constructing a framework of canes, tennis balls and acres of netting, Blackie has been helping himself to the crop. He waits until Clive has unfurled enough of the netting to crawl in among the bushes and then hops in after him. Chasing him is a tiring and largely fruitless exercise (pun intended).

Meanwhile, the set of pans he ordered (Clive, that is, not Blackie) for the all-grain brewing project arrives. I wonder where he is planning to store them.

# JULY

## 1 July

Our local Buddhists at the Nagarjuna Kadampa Meditation Centre hold a summer fete every year and we usually go. I've been to several weekend retreats and courses there; Clive restricts himself to the free 20-minute meditation session once every 12 months. It's usually a good do, but this year it's a bit of a disappointment, in part because it has become a victim of its own success. There are just too many people and not enough places to get a drink in the sweltering 30-

degree heat. Not only that, but also there are only so many stalls of crystals, ting-sha and incense you can look at, and the atmosphere isn't conducive to a massage or Reiki treatment. We stay long enough to buy a book, *The Native People of Alaska* (because you never know when you might need to know why an Inapuit woman would offer a drink of water to a dead whale), a jar of extremely expensive honey and, inevitably, some joss sticks.

### 2 July

Clive surprises me this morning by declaring he'd like to do some yoga. I do a practice every morning before breakfast to set the tone for my day and often say, 'Join me?' and he has until now always replied, 'Not today.' This morning, though, he says he'll give it a go. I find a beginner session on YouTube and to my astonishment he does it.

In other news: 'The bastard blackbird's been at it again.'

### 3 July

The lump sum of the pension arrives. This means that we can now pay off the last £4,000-ish of our mortgage. Let joy be unconfined.

### 4 July

No yoga for Clive this morning. Instead he rises early and sets about all-grain brewing with his shiny new pans. This means the whole house now smells like, well, like a brewery.

## 5 July

The heatwave continues, but Clive keeps plodding up to the allotment at the top and tail ends of the day. This morning, though, he declares that the leeks just can't wait any longer and sets off to plant them. They were started off at home in seed trays, then thinned out so the stronger ones could grow on unimpeded by their weaker siblings. In the meantime we have been collecting toilet roll tubes, so that each plant can be planted into its own cardboard cocoon to protect it from the slugs and dirt. It's very disheartening to pull up a leek only to find its layers interspersed with tenacious grit. (Good name for a band, by the way: *Please welcome on stage – Tenacious Grit!*)

After a couple of hours' graft, Clive decides he needs a bit of a rest in the shade. The sun is overhead by now, so the only sanctuary is in the shed, where he settles himself down on a pile of cardboard, has a drink, then closes his eyes, just for a moment. He wakes up an hour later, temporarily bewildered by his surroundings.

## 6 July

Today, Clive, Sam and Joe have gone to Thorpe Park for some rollercoaster-based fun. I am invited, but decline. I don't want to go to spend the day holding the bottles of water while they hurtle around defying gravity. I'm too much of a control freak to get the value out of my ticket price and I don't enjoy being scared witless. The boys hide their disappointment well.

## 7 July

Our good friend Ian and his new wife are throwing a party today to celebrate the 200th anniversary of 'Colombian Press No.13'. Ian is a renowned wood engraver and this machine is his printing press, a magnificent beast of a thing designed by inventor George Clymer of Philadelphia. It is an interesting afternoon, populated by a quirky, arty guest list, some of whom we instantly take to, others that we are frankly bemused by.

Then it is home to watch the football: England 2, Sweden 0. We're in the semi-finals!

## 8 July

Man, it's hot! Neither of us wants to move very far, so we don't. I spend the afternoon with Jack Reacher, and Clive alternates between mooching and pottering. If this is what weekends are like in retirement, I'm all for it.

## 9 July

Today we both do our own thing: word-wrangling for me and currant-crushing for Clive. I keep saying we've got too many soft fruit bushes, but apparently I'm wrong. Either way, it's not my problem: I'm not the one who has to grub about on hands and knees picking the damn things.

The evening sees us swanning off to the Stahl Theatre for the Oundle International Festival, to see Kabantu, a group of extraordinary young musicians described in the programme as 'reinventors of global sounds, rewriters of rulebooks'. Yep, that just about covers it. It is a great evening. Despite us never having been there before, there are two people in the audience we know. Actually, there is one I know and another who recognises me from a performance of the Deep Roots Tall Trees dancetheatre of which I am a member. *'Mama, don't worry about me, I'm nearly famous now.'*

### 10 July

We might be officially mortgage free, but Clive is still checking the bank balance every morning. His *Mastermind* specialist subject would definitely be Excel spreadsheets. I'm glad he's keeping an eye on things, but I can't imagine anything much has happened since yesterday. This might become 'a thing' if I let it.

### 11 July

Not much to report today. More currants, more courgettes, yet more currants. Oh, and England are out of the World Cup, losing 2-1 to Croatia.

## 12 July

I can't remember the last time I was this busy, which is great, of course. The devil makes work for idle writers. With the best of intentions, Clive hovers (there is no other word for it), trying to be helpful, but there isn't anything he can do; he can't spell and I can't make pastry, so life works best when we stick to our individual strengths. Today, he really gets on my nerves, but this isn't his fault, poor man.

My mood isn't helped by a ridiculous pop-up thing that keeps appearing on my screen and slows my processor down to the speed of an arthritic sloth. Eventually I download something called Malwarebytes, which seems to do the trick, but it means I have a grumpy start and the mood never leaves me.

## 13 July

Clive wisely gives me a wide berth today.

## 14 July

KettFest starts in earnest today. This is our local celebration of the arts and culture in all its guises. It's a great idea, but it hasn't really taken off and goes on in spite of the townsfolk, rather than because of them. Nevertheless, I play my part by running a creative writing activity in the library for a small but enthusiastic group. Then in the afternoon I take part in a spoken word event in a courtyard that was far too hot. Clive earns my appreciation by acting as my roadie.

His reward is to be my plus-one at a swanky party in the evening. Pimms on arrival, canapés everywhere we turn, flunkies in attendance to top up our drinks, topiary, dancing, hog roast, more drink. It is a swelligant, elegant party of the highest order. We only know a few people, but, suitably lubricated, everyone is very friendly. Of course, as soon as they find out Clive is recently retired, they have plenty of advice to offer. (The guests were all of an age, you might say.) The women generally offer me sympathy, while the men rally round Clive saying that it is the best thing he could have done, and he should join this club or take up that hobby. The U3A is mentioned, as it often is in such conversations. One chap suggests an MA in Astrophysics. Now, that I'd like to see.

**15 July**
It's St Swithin's Day, but there's no sign of rain. It's been weeks now, and our garden is looking very sorry for itself. It's a good job Clive has plenty of time for watering from our enormous water butts. Today's haul from the allotment: six courgettes, five beetroots and a solitary onion.

**16 July**
My home office is actually one end of an extension that runs along the back of our house. When we're feeling pretentious we call it the Garden Room. The other end gets used for whatever the season demands. When the

boys were little and Joe was busy 'keeping it tight at the back' playing in deep defence for Weekley Rovers FC, the place was filled with footballs, boots, cones and other soccer-related paraphernalia. The house still reflects the age of its occupants. As I look across now, I can see a huge bag of birdseed, a bag of shredded paper waiting to be added to the compost bin, two well-used garden chairs and Clive's discarded slippers, flattened at the heel end because it takes him too long to put them on properly.

Until recently there have also been three demijohns of in-progress blackcurrant wine. However, I don't know whether it's the heat or simply over-enthusiasm, but one of them has erupted in Eyjafjallajökull style, disgorging sweet stickiness all over the Porcelanosa. It makes me wonder if my recent lethargy has been caused not by the heat, but by alcoholic fumes escaping from the airlocks.

## 17 July

Clive has discovered a new sense of freedom can be achieved by doing housework in just his boxers and a t-shirt. It's fine, honestly. I mean, it's hot and he's messy, so in a way it makes sense. It's not as though he ever comes perilously close to setting off to post a letter without putting this trousers on. Oh, wait.

Later that same day… In the distance, I can hear him saying, 'No,' time after time, with increasing weariness. Fearing he's having some sort of episode, I track him down. He is on the phone to a robot, by which I mean he is grappling with the intricacies of internet banking. An automated system is putting him through his paces to ascertain which human he needs to speak to, assuming he passes muster. There is clearly a change of tactic at the other end, because suddenly Clive is saying, 'My voice is my password,' firmly but calmly at first, but then rising in pitch and volume until he eventually adds the phrase, 'You stupid bint!' This doesn't help.

It puts me in mind of an Eddie Izzard skit from many years ago where he talks about the futility of early French lessons. He tells a typically convoluted anecdote that involves him repeating the phrase, 'Mais le singe est dans l'arbre.'

I am *this close* to suggesting Clive try: 'Mais ma voix est mon mot de passe.'

## 18 July

No one keeps me calm like Clive and today he does sterling work. It is the launch do for my book *Stripped-back Yoga*, and I am convinced no one will turn up. He just keeps saying, 'It'll be fine. More tea?'

And of course he is right – although there are people who had said they would come but don't. I make a note of their names. Sam comes, too, and distinguishes himself by being the only person to have the nous to buy a pint at the bar, eschewing the virtuously presented fruit juice and cordial I had organised, what with it being a yoga thing and all. Nothing to do with budgetary restrictions. (£35 for a bottle of Prosecco? I don't think so!)

**19 July**
Today is a CBA kind of day. Not, as you might be thinking, Could Be Awesome, but rather Can't Be Arsed. Clive manages to stay busy doing nothing all day, save for hanging a picture, peeling and freezing a pound of broad beans and posting a letter. I suppose he deserves it after yesterday.

**20 July**
I have the house to myself for most of the day, because Clive is off to Stansted to deliver Joe and Caitlin as they set off for a holiday somewhere hot. I get loads of stuff done. In the evening we go to see *The Crucible* in Northampton, because our friend Will is playing Giles Corey. A splendid, if sticky evening. There is a bit of a thunderstorm while we are inside, but driving the 17 or so miles back home it becomes clear that the rain was very localised and Kettering is still parched. Will it ever rain again?

**21 July**
Today promises to be a good day for both of us, because we are doing our own thing. I go to Stamford for a ukulele course, leaving his lordship at home to do I know not what. I have a lovely day and am in the mood for a lovely evening, too.

When I open the door, Clive is making his way gingerly down the stairs without his trousers. It turns out that his first job of the day – to go to the supermarket – was also his last, as he'd tripped over the kerb and buggered his knee. I know he hasn't done this on purpose: but way to spoil the mood. He's made a pretty poor job of buying the food, too.

The evening is spent with much sighing. No one milks an injury like a mardy man. He declares himself too shaken to eat: 'It must be the shock.' I make do with a can of Heinz finest Cream of Tomato. When I started writing this book, I had visions of recording amusing anecdotes and moments of whimsy. Today it's not funny. Not funny at all.

## 22 July

A penitent Clive is doing his best to appease me today, but I'm not in the mood. Instead I am wielding the Mr Sheen in an overly flamboyant way. The air is thick with the smell of burning martyr.

## 23 July

An unintended consequence of Clive's retirement is that I have put on weight. This isn't fair. I'm putting it down to stress and not all those Magnum Mini ice-creams. Nor is it fair that while I'm sitting at my screen trying to earn a living in 30-degree heat, with my buttocks sticking to my chair, he retires to the coolest room in the house to catch up with last night's round of the Tour de France.

This evening's picking session at the allotment brought forth more courgettes (naturally), a bagful of spinach and the first of the runner beans. What began on 25 June continues.

## 24 July

Virgin is doing something mysterious to our internet connection today, so we have a tech-free morning, which is rather lovely. It comes back on at lunchtime, but by then we've already decided to take it easy. I do some vague admin and then go to Weaving Words, my weekly writing group. It is the last one before our summer break and we use seaside postcards as our main prompt, while we drink mocktails decorated with fruit slices and fresh mint. I swallow a lemon pip, but try not to let it show.

Clive manipulates the currant wines and then settles down to watch what looks to me like a terrible film: *Pixels*. It stars Adam Sandler, which is usually all I need to know to avoid it. On the plus side, it didn't have Nicolas Cage in it.

## 25 July

The BBC assures us that the weather will break on Friday. In the meantime, we fuddle our way through the day trying not to move too quickly. While I stay inside grappling with uploading e-versions of *Stripped-back*

*Yoga*, Clive has opened a tin of wood preservative and set about titivating the back gate. I've just checked what colour it was, in the hope that it would be something amusing like Hobbit's Whiskers or Beaver's Delight. It is labelled Dark Brown. How disappointing.

## 26 July

We continue to huff and puff today, as the in-car thermometer records 34°C. I check my coordinates to make sure I haven't fallen through a tear in the time-space continuum and landed in Alicante. Neither of us sleeps well. Clive decides to take a moment in front of the telly downstairs while I toss and turn upstairs. When I come down an hour or so later, I find him on the living room floor in the foetal position in front of News 24, still awake. Partial respite comes at about 3am, when there is a burst of thunder and lightning and a modest amount of rain. The temperature doesn't drop.

## 27 July

After a burst of enthusiasm with the polish, Clive goes upstairs to wash and change. Half an hour later, I find him asleep on our bed. Bless him.

We should have been observing a Blood Moon this evening, caused by the total eclipse of the Moon by the Earth. Unfortunately, it was cloudy and we couldn't see anything at all.

## 28 July

I teach a yoga class this morning at Rothwell Methodist Church, the last event to publicise *Stripped-back Yoga*. It goes well, but for the rest of the day I am in a bit of a zombie state. I think the last month has finally caught up with me, because all I want to do is sit about. Clive starts the day with an USDAW meeting, then joins me in mostly pottering.

## 29 July

Nothing much to report, on a day filled with more laziness or recharging of the batteries, depending on your point of view.

## 30 July

Clive has been saying he was a bit disappointed that we hadn't managed any weekday outings since he gave up work, so today I put an 'out of office' message on my email account and off we go. We take a trip to West Hunsbury Country Park, which is only just the other side of Northampton and yet we've never been there before. There was an Iron Age hill fort here, and you can walk round the outline of the ditch and hilltop. We extend our walk to the lake and make a big circle back to the Drover's Return café for the most enormous sandwiches and mugs of tea. The owner has a ukulele behind the counter, so I tune it up and have a bit of a play. There's a disused railway track there, too, with a museum (which wasn't open), celebrating the quarrying

34

that used to go on there. No one does heritage like the Brits do.

Clive is right, of course. This is what we should be doing more of. It is a good day.

## 31 July

Golf today. Him, of course, not me. I've swung a club in anger at the driving range a couple of times and I'm a demon when it comes to putting a ball through the legs of a clay giraffe or down the plank of a pirate ship, but I've never fancied taking up the proper game. I wonder if it's because my brothers and father all played and I got fed up of it, even before I understood what it was all about.

So notwithstanding the heat, Clive and Paul go off for nine holes. It is important, he tells me, to get his eye in ahead of the golf trip next week. Yes, they did finally manage to book something and they're off to Norfolk for five days. His trip away will do us both good.

# AUGUST

## 1 August

Joe and Caitlin are due to return from Fuerteventura today. Clive is picking them up from Stansted later and is reluctant to expend any energy ahead of the drive. Fair enough. He has to be there at one o'clock in the morning, which I suppose is technically tomorrow.

I teach a sticky class centred on krounchasana, the heron pose. Then I spend the afternoon in an editing frenzy, before going to a private view at the Rooftop Gallery in Corby, followed by a dancetheatre rehearsal.

The first royalty payment arrives for *Stripped-back Yoga*: £6.99. I celebrate with a Toffee Crisp.

## 2 August

Lunch with my good friend Will today, he who was in *The Crucible*. We call these get-togethers business meetings, because years ago I was his secretary and now we are both freelances, but although we compare notes on our various projects it's really just nice to catch up. Today I try not to be envious of his holiday plans; he is off to America. After my working day it is ukulele practice, which is great fun. I like it when I can play the songs, which isn't always the case. Clive does little, recovering from the Stansted trip.

## 3 August

I go to Melton Mowbray to meet up with Jeanette, who did the yoga teacher training with me. We bonded in kindred bafflement during most of the course and became good friends. I take her a copy of *Stripped-back Yoga*, which she starts to read immediately and is kind enough to say lovely things about. While I am out, Clive discovers we have a cable TV channel called Sky Sports Mix. Oh dear.

## 4 August

After a fabulous day at a yoga retreat with some good friends, I find myself unnecessarily annoyed at Clive's lack of activity. We've already established I can be a bit of a martyr (see 22 July, for instance), but the fact that he is a bit under the weather doesn't wash with me. We have words.

Meanwhile, I get a random email from my mother with 'Query' in the subject line and the simple message: 'Do you know how I can get on to something called "drop box"?' Now what's she up to?

## 5 August

We learn that Barry Chuckle has died, the older of the two Chuckle Brothers. Shame. Mind you, I was too old to appreciate their humour and my children too young; but their shows fall into the general category of 'mostly harmless', as Douglas Adams might have said.

We take a trip today to the Bardic Picnic in Northampton, which is every bit as weird as might be expected. There is much poetry and music, far too much exposed flesh and just the right amount of vegan ice-cream. The new Bard is announced as Sami Stuart E Tite, an interesting character who I'm sure will bring colour to the role. Also, mostly harmless, I suspect.

## 6 August

There's a cheque for £2,000 in the post this morning. Thank you, HMRC.

## 7 August

The new bathroom scales are misbehaving. Obviously we all think the numbers are wrong, but twice now I've got on them to be told I'm a pound over my absolutely-can't-get-any-heavier limit. The thing is, though, that if I get off and then on again, my weight goes down by three pounds. Clive says the same. We conduct an experiment. Clive stands on the scales; we note the weight. (How much?!) He gets off and then back on again, this time while holding a 2lb weight. The numbers go down. A trip to Dunelm Mill to return them proves satisfactory. Unfortunately, standing on the replacement scales shows consistently that we both need to take a close look at our input:output ratio.

**8 August**
Like an excited schoolboy off to his first camp, Clive sets off for Norfolk with Paul and Frank for their golf trip. Along with plenty of cash for the beer kitty and a fresh pack of Rennies for the inevitable overindulgence, Clive has taken a spreadsheet of all the scores from their previous encounters. It makes me smile how seriously they take it all, even going to the trouble of having physical trophies for the overall weekend winner, the wooden spoon for the loser and the broken club for the highest number of shots taken on one hole. It could be worse; they could be off to Vegas with the housekeeping money. Paul is on the phone early to say he and Frank are packed and ready, so can Clive meet them earlier than planned? I try not to be offended by the alacrity with which he skips off.

Later that evening, I distinguish myself in dance theatre rehearsals by splitting my trousers during an overenthusiastic warm-up routine, and spend the rest of the evening trying to move with my back to the wall.

## 9 August

I'm always slightly anxious when Clive goes away because it means I am left in sole charge of the fish tank. I avoid counting the little critters, so I shall be in blissful ignorance should one or more of them die. When I was a child I had a goldfish who drowned. You will, then, understand my nervousness. I'm also in charge of watering not only the garden, but also the allotment. This won't be a problem this evening, because we had a torrential downpour this morning, although it's still very warm.

On the topic of the allotment, Ros, in whose beautiful home I teach yoga on Thursday mornings, sends me away with a big bag of alpaca poo today, which I'm sure Clive will appreciate when he returns.

## 10 August

Taking advantage of a cancelled meeting and an unexpected clear day, I drive to Staffordshire to see Mum. Once we've caught up on family news, we put the world to rights. Despite not being quite on the same political page, we rarely fall out during our lively discussions of such matters as Boris Johnson, Brexit, gay clergy, councils or the dearth of decent programmes on TV. We have a little tinkle on the piano and the ukulele, then I drive home. The A50 is a nightmare, even by its low standards.

I get a text from Clive, who is, apparently, missing me. Aw, shucks.

## 11 August
My plans for blitzing the house in Clive's absence have come to nought. I meet Alison in town, a woman I first encountered through work but who has become a friend. She is a whirlwind of ideas and might need my input for some of her forthcoming plans. I'm looking forward to that, because she is delightful to work with.

I dutifully trot up to the allotment later in the day, where I discover that Thursday's downpour has caused a growth spurt on the courgette bed, where specimens of the most extraordinary girth await me.

## 12 August
The hero has returned tired but happy, golf trophy in hand, as overall winner for the sixth time. He has a very red triangle peeping out from the top of his polo-shirt from where the sun has caught him.

## 13 August
Despite his lovely trip away, or perhaps because of it, Clive is in thoughtful mood today, confessing that it is as I feared and he is worried about having no one to play with while I'm at work. My suggestions that he

should seek out other golf partners or, heaven forbid, join something are not well received. I'm not sure what we're going to do about this. I would love to retire, too, but that is some years off. In the meantime, I will try to organise myself to free up a bit more time for Clive's anticipated trips out. Some deep thinking is required.

**14 August**

It seems that Clive is the one doing the thinking. He is suspiciously quiet and as I look over his shoulder I catch him looking at the U3A website. I make no comment, but notice that he seems to have reached C on the list of interest groups on offer, where, inter alia, there are two concerned with card-making, an occupation I've never understood and shall actively dissuade him from, should he be tempted.

**15 August**

As he sets off for the allotment today, I ask Clive to come back with a cheery anecdote to brighten my day. (I am proofreading *Logistics & Transport Focus*, which is a fine publication, but today isn't particularly engaging.) He returns with no hilarious stories, but does have a couple of bags of veg in which there is, rather inevitably, an amusing carrot resembling a little man with ill-matched legs and puny genitals. I think I might have dated the original in my youth. Apparently the Red Arrows flew over the plot in two groups of five aircraft, and later we had a Spitfire over our garden. Is something going on we should be worried about?

## 16 August
I'm tempted to say that Clive is winding down towards the weekend, but he hasn't really wound up since he came back from his golf trip.

'Well,' he says, 'it's hardly worth it.'

We are going away together on Saturday. I grind my teeth and type faster.

## 17 August
Joe comes round to take instruction on how to look after the tomato plants while we are away. I suspect that he will largely ignore the details and just turn the hose on everything. Works for me.

## 18 August
Having resigned ourselves to a ten-hour drive to Cornwall, we are pleasantly surprised to do the journey in seven. This is due in part to the satnav suggesting a detour that I am reluctant to follow, but that actually saves us time. To his credit, Clive resists saying, 'I told you so,' and I have to admit there is something very satisfying about watching the on-screen estimated time of arrival drawing closer.

Our holiday cottage, a barn conversion in St Buryan (home of John Le Carré, apparently) is very nice, but there is absolutely no phone signal and not a hint of internet connection. This is fine by me, because I'm still resolutely refusing to use a smartphone and I'm happy to be uncontactable for a week. Clive, though, keeps checking, as though if he sneaks up on Virgin it might let him make a phone call. In the end I have to warn him not to keep saying, 'No, there's no signal.' It's that, or he has to sleep in the car.

## 19 August

We set off to explore the Cornish lanes. ('Still no signal.')

We drive along enjoying the scenery. Suddenly Clive says, 'Oh look, a winery.' I mishear this as, 'Oh look, a library,' and there in a nutshell is the chalk and cheese on which our relationship is built.

We go to Godolphin Gardens, a National Trust property, where a wonderful guide takes us around the grounds regaling us with tales of a hapless builder called Malcolm who was responsible for huge dollops of concrete on the slate roofs and otherwise beautiful stonework of the listed buildings. Later, in the teashop, an unpleasant family allow their son Austin to open and close the door time after time after time. I'm itching to clip him round the ear, but Clive distracts me with the thought that perhaps the lad is missing his brother Healey, or possibly Allegro.

We call into Mousehole on our way back where an altogether more acceptable child is clambering all over the rocks, falling over often, but always scrambling back to his feet with a cheery 'I'm OK!' This makes my day.

## 20 August

It's a murky morning, but we stick to our plan and head off to the old Levant tin mine, another National Trust property. We park at nearby Geevor and walk the short distance across a rather terrifying landscape where redundant chimneys loom out of the mist. I am most disconcerted – and it is even worse on the way back! The place is worth the trip, though, and we have another excellent guide. A couple from New Zealand join our group late and proceed to ask questions that have already been answered, then corner the guide for a personal Q&A session that holds everyone up.

Afterwards, as we sit eating our pasties, there is much discussion as to whether the moisture in the air is low cloud, sea mist or actual rain. Whatever. As the middle distance disappears, we abandon our plans to walk out down the coast and scurry back to our cottage to watch films and eat chocolate.

## 21 August

Better weather today, so we head off to Chysauster, to see the remains of a Romano-British village. This one is English Heritage, because we like to spread our middle-class largesse. On the way we spot the Tremenheere Sculpture Park, which proves to be an unexpected delight. We decide we are as qualified as anyone there to express an opinion on the works, given that we both have a BS in Art Appreciation.

Needing to clear our heads, we head to Newlyn and spend a happy hour picking up pebbles.

## 22 August

It has to be done. Despite our misgivings about rampant commercialism, we make a trip to Land's End and are pleasantly surprised. Clive accesses his inner child with ease, as we buy a ticket for all four of the family attractions. We begin in 'Return to the Lost World', a 4D film show clearly aimed at kids, complete with vibrating chairs, squirting water and bubbles. Then it's on to 'Aardman Presents: A Grand Experience', where Clive has his photo taken with Wallace and Gromit (he's 63, for heaven's sake). The 'Arthur's Quest' mirror maze bamboozles us completely, but fortunately the Greeb Farm petting zoo isn't far away, where we hold our noses around the goat pens and marvel at the antics of the ducks. Simple pleasures. We do also go and look at the actual end of the land and have a grand walk along the coast.

Before we leave, there's just time for a look in the gift shop. Clive buys a couple of bottles of beer for Malcolm, who is watering the allotment for him, and gets into quite a conversation with the lad behind the counter. When I hear him start to reminisce about his late mother's penchant for gin, I decide it's time to drag him away.

## 23 August

In 1984, my family went to the Leicester Haymarket Theatre to see *Me And My Girl*. This was the production based on Stephen Fry's revision of the original book and ahead of its transfer to the Adelphi in London's glittering West End. It was a wonderful evening and we all came home singing. Today, we are off to the fabulous outdoor Minack Theatre to see The Mitre Players' production of this same musical. We conclude that it might have lacked the tap-dancing prowess of Robert Lindsay and Emma Thompson, who played the leads Bill Snibson and Sally Smith in the Leicester version, but Paul Grace and Megan Brown did a great job in the roles. Once again, we come home singing.

While we are waiting to go into the theatre we stand around reading the information boards, and are amazed to be joined by someone we know: Joe and Sam's former Cub Scout leader. Clive often comments that wherever we go I see someone we know, but at 330 miles from home this has to be a record.

That evening, dozing on the sofa and flicking through the TV channels, we happen upon *The Great British Menu*, just in time to hear a judge say, 'At last you've told a story with your dessert.' What times we live in.

## 24 August

Our last day on holiday, and we head for St Michael's Mount. The tide is low, so we walk across the causeway and, later, get the little boat back. It's very beautiful and we fall into silent reverie. After a while Clive says, 'I think granite is my favourite rock.' He is affronted that this makes me laugh.

We call in at Penzance on the way back and wish we hadn't bothered. It's horrible.

## 25 August

With heavy hearts we set off home along the notorious A30, but once again the traffic gods are with us and we make such good time that we are home in time to pop into The Yards Bar, where Joe has organised the bands for the evening, including his own. It's always good to see him playing live. Sam is there and Caitlin, of course, and a fairly large contingent of Caitlin's family (who shall henceforth be known as the Hunter Gathering). This is a surprise, and if I'd known they were going to be there I might have taken the time to put on a bit of slap. A good time is had by all and we sleep well that night. All that sea air and the long drive, don't you know; nothing to do with the beer. Oh no.

## 26 August

It's pouring with rain. With a touch of the post-holiday blues, we set to with some half-hearted domestic duties, but eventually capitulate and spend the day watching old episodes of *ER* and sighing quite a bit. Clive gets busy with his beloved spreadsheets and declares that we are still solvent, which is reassuring.

## 27 August

It's a Bank Holiday and the sun is out, so we set off for a walk along the Lyveden Way, which takes in Lyveden New Bield, our nearest National Trust property and a place we know well. It was designed by Sir Thomas Tresham, a man who incorporated Catholic symbolism into all his projects. The garden lodge at Lyveden was intended to stand as a testament of his faith despite the dramatic changes that were going on at the time – this was Elizabethan England – but it was never completed. He was imprisoned and the builders scarpered when they realised they weren't going to get paid.

We pick up more pebbles. Some 20-odd years ago, when Clive was studying for his OU degree in Natural Sciences, I bought him a rock tumbler, a curious device that turns pebbles into, well, shiny pebbles. He only used it once. Now he has decided it's time to resurrect it and, armed with the samples from Newlyn and a few from today's walk, he has it up and running in the spare bedroom. It's quite a noisy contraption, as you might imagine. You know that sound you get when you've left some coins in your pocket when you put your jeans in the washing-machine? Yes, that. He's put the tumbler on one of my old yoga blocks and actually it's not too bad, but lying in the bath that night I am aware of the *kerchunk-slosh* from the adjacent room. The writer in me is pleased to have learned a new word: lapidary – an artist or artisan who forms stone, minerals or gemstones into decorative items. Every day's a school day.

## 28 August

Bad news from the allotment where the wasps have savaged the sweetcorn crop. Worse, though, is that we've had intruders in the field some time over the weekend. When we took on our plot, Russell, who is in charge, advised us not to bother locking our shed and to take anything valuable to and fro, and while it is a bit of a pain to load and unload every trip, this has proved to be good advice. The theory is that if someone does get in, at best they'll go off with a few plant pots and they won't have to break off the lock in the process. Sadly for our lovely plot-neighbour Malcolm, his beautiful wooden building – it's too grand to be dismissed as a mere shed – has been broken into, and in the process the thieves have broken down his door. Not only that, but they have also taken his new mower. What's wrong with people?

## 29 August

More intruders up at the field. Our shed was opened and the secateurs have disappeared, but there is every chance they will reveal themselves when we pull up the courgette triffids at the end of the season. Otherwise everything is there and undamaged. Rumours are rife as to who is responsible. One theory is that it's an inside job, given that specific sheds seem to have been targeted where the best equipment is kept, and that the cut-through chain on the gate is a ploy to throw the police off the scent. There is apparently a relative newcomer whom some have described as looking 'a bit of a wrong 'un'. The other notion is that it's a real coincidence that these invasions have happened just as a load of travellers have set up camp on the nearby park. It shames us both that we consider this option without a scrap of evidence.

**30 August**

The first batch of pebbles comes to the end of its initial tumbling today, amid much excitement. I'm poking a little gentle fun, but actually I'm almost as intrigued as Clive to see how they've changed. It's incredible, I kid you not. Already, subtle colours have revealed themselves and I start to see the appeal of this hobby. I'm still not sure what we're supposed to do with the finished items, but no doubt there's a plan of which I've yet to be informed. The stones are rinsed and returned for a second tumbling. It might be my imagination, but the *kerchunk* seems to be getting louder.

**31 August**

Brewing update. There are three demijohns of newly racked-off blackcurrant wine in the spare bedroom with the potential to make about 18 bottles. Meanwhile, on the kitchen table there is a fermentation bucket full of first-stage mixed fruit wine: more blackcurrants, some redcurrants and apples from our garden. This, too, will become about 18 bottles of loveliness.

The next project will be a kit of Founding Father Pale Ale (a mere 40 pints). This particular kit is a commemorative beer created to celebrate the life of Philip Jones, who developed all the original Festival beer kits. He died in 2014 at the stupidly young age of 52, but had been a supporter of Ugandan Children's Charity Medcare, so the price of each pack of this brew kit includes a donation to the charity.

Then there'll be another SMaSH brew, for which Clive has bought a tub of coarse ground Irish moss. When I saw it I thought it might be for use on the garden, but no; apparently it 'improves precipitation of proteins during the wort boil'. Well, there's a thing.

Wort, as I'm sure you know, is the liquid obtained when malt enzymes attach a heated aqueous slurry of ground endosperm of malted and unmalted cereal. None the wiser? Me neither. I've just looked it up on an online glossary. I've also learned that the haze that sometimes appears in said wort is called trub. I'm not a big fan of business jargon – blue-sky thinking, drilling down, going forward – but there's something about hobby-specific words that is rather pleasing and home brewing has some lovely ones, among them hop nose, lautering, rousing, spile and testcock.

# SEPTEMBER

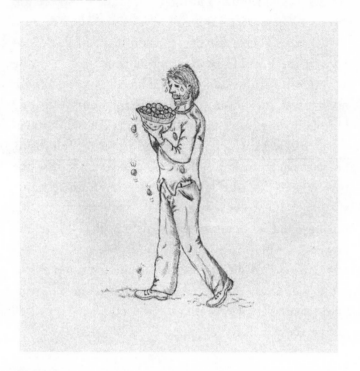

## 1 September

Summer is clinging on by its fingernails, but our tubs are looking a bit sad, so we pop up to Bosworths Garden Centre to buy a bit of autumn colour. We come home with mini cyclamens and some blue plants that lose their label before we get home, so I don't know what they are. No matter. I bodge them into the compost with my usual finesse. Clive is determined to resurrect that patch of brown earth that used to be our lawn and fully intends to scarify the whole thing, but we are due at the theatre and there isn't time to do the job justice, so he postpones it.

We have tickets for the opening night of *The Lovely Bones* at the Royal in Northampton, which proves to be a wonderful show. It's a 90-minute performance with no interval and some of the audience shift from one buttock to the other towards the end. We oldies moan about the lack of attention span the young folk have, but our age group can be just as bad. Added to this, the two women to our left spend most of the evening sharing a huge bag of Maltesers, with the inevitable rustling and chomping that this entails. When the powers that be finally put me in charge – and it's surely only a matter of time – I shall ban the consumption of food and drink in theatres and cinemas, and anyone who leaves part way through for a comfort break will not be allowed back in.

## 2 September
This evening we go to dinner with a group of people we met through the National Childbirth Trust. We 'girls' meet fairly regularly, but this is the first time we can remember all five couples being together, despite the children that brought us together in the first place now approaching 30. We remark on how unusual we are, given that we all still have the partners we started out with. It's a pot luck supper, each of us having contributed something to the feast. As the only vegetarian in the party, I come home slightly peckish.

During the course of the evening, Clive chats to Pete (who has retired but is off to New Zealand for seven months to take up a locum GP position) and Robin (slightly younger and with a few years to go before he can think of packing up work). They compare notes on their various situations. Pete is surprised that Clive was given no counselling by his firm and passes on some advice given to him: find eight things to do, namely two outside on your own, two outside with someone else, two inside on your own and two inside with someone else. I think it's fair to say this is a work in progress.

One other suggestion was to take up bowls. Apparently this seemingly refined pastime is a hotbed of wife-swapping. (Insert your own 'wood' joke here.)

## 3 September

There is a green light flashing on the router, but since everything is apparently working we decide to ignore it.

Technology might be more or less under control, but the mechanical devices are fighting back today. Building on Saturday's mow, with the blades set appropriately, the electric scarifier is brought out of the shed, but refuses to cooperate. After a certain amount of faffing, Clive remembers that he has a collection of widgets and doobries in a rucksack in the shed, and for a few moments he trundles up and down the lawn collecting thatch. Suddenly silence descends and I look up from my desk to see him scratching his head. Something has gone awry and the belt that holds the doodah to the thingummy has risen up and scored a line through the whatchamacallit. Long story short, parts have to be sourced online.

Meanwhile, upstairs the tumbler has stopped. This is put down to too much grease on the spindles, and sure enough, after a bit of a wipe it resumes its business.

## 4 September

The tumbler has stopped again and this time it's more serious: the belt has snapped. This means the cylinders have to be emptied and the liquor therein disposed of on to the gravel behind the shed; it will solidify so mustn't be put down the plughole. There is a certain amount of sighing, but I point out that this hiccup doesn't matter in the great scheme of things. For some reason, this doesn't help.

Later, as I beaver away typing something magnificent, Clive plugs in the heater for the fermentation vessel full of fruit wine. My computer goes off, along with everything else connected to a downstairs socket. I am not best pleased.

## 5 September

Wednesday is pensioner day at B&Q, so while I'm out teaching a yoga class Clive trots off to buy some woodstain to revitalise the front door.

The Founding Father is bubbling away nicely in the space under the stairs, wrapped in an old sleeping-bag to keep it toastie. It sounds like a bilious uncle.

## 6 September

A friend who has been retired for well over a year has been asked by his old firm if he'd like to go back on the basis of choosing his own hours and pretty much name his price. He says he's tempted, but it sounds like a terrible idea to me.

It's flattering to be asked, of course, and he might find the money useful (not that he's short of a bob or two), but he's been pleasing himself for long enough now to find it impossible to slot back into a formal work environment, surely. I occasionally drop into offices to pick up or drop off some work, and I'm always glad to come home. It's as though while I'm in the business environment I have to hold my breath and it's only when I'm back in the sanctuary of my desk at home that I can exhale again. It's none of my business, but I'd stay where I am if I were him.

## 7 September

By lunchtime today I've met all my work targets, so on a whim we set off for a walk. We go to Lyveden New Bield again, but this time instead of following the marked footpath through Fermyn Woods we go the other way. The seven-mile loop takes us to the village of Wadenhoe and is largely in woodland. Clive has a fitness app on his phone through which some woman keeps saying 'Workout paused' every time we stop to check the map or take a swig of water. This makes us feel as though we've been naughty. She does, though, say 'Workout resumed' when we get going again, and gives us regular updates on how far we've walked. We get a little fanfare after four miles, which is nice.

This is a good day.

## 8 September

This is a bad day. The best-laid plans certainly 'gang aft agley'. It is too painful to recall in detail. Suffice to say that one of us is driving the car as we set off in the wrong direction for a trip out to a nearby town; one of us forgets the money-off tokens that prompted the trip in the first place; one of us gets a parking ticket by (a) leaving the ticket we'd paid for upside-down on the dashboard, so it looks as though we might be trying to pull a fast one and (b) putting the wrong registration number on the ticket, so it definitely looks as though we're trying to pull a fast one; one of us spends the afternoon on the sofa in a sulk; one of us stomps about in the kitchen, ostentatiously cooking a meal that is, frankly, disgusting (you wouldn't think it possible to cook a biryani in which the rice is congealed but the vegetables are raw); one of us brings the day to a grand finale by knocking over a glass of red wine on to the light-coloured carpet.

## 9 September

Divorce lawyers are expensive, so we decide instead to pretend yesterday never happened and manage to pass the day in relative harmony, albeit with not inconsiderable effort. We do a sort of 'After-you-no-after-you' dance.

We go for an urban walk, taking our life into our hands and negotiating the nearby retail park on foot in an environment definitely not designed with pedestrians in mind. I need to buy a travel alarm clock to use in my yoga classes. I use it to keep track of the time, not to wake them up at the end. Then we mooch on to Sports Direct, where Clive tries on about 500 pairs of walking trainers before settling on some he likes. It's probably coincidence, but after this shopping trip we both start to itch. Investigation reveals that we are both suffering from insect bites. I won't say fleas.

The afternoon is spent making green tomato chutney and preparing little onions for pickling. These will be put aside until Boxing Day lunchtime, when they will be brought out to accompany cold turkey, leftover chipolatas, chips and bubble and squeak. We know how to live.

## 10 September

The new trainers don't fit. The receipt has been shredded, so they can't be changed. I sigh.

As well as the trainers, we bought some new darts yesterday and had a couple of games in the afternoon. We are both rubbish at it, and end up needing double sixteen, then double eight, then double four, then double two, then, inevitably, double one. This morning we both get up with an ache in our right biceps. Good grief, how old are we!

Sam pops in for lunch sporting a new haircut. He is blessed with lovely blond locks that he tends to grow until they annoy him, then he goes to the Kurdish barber in town. Apparently conversation is sparse, usually consisting of 'Haircut? Sit,' followed some time later by a request for payment. Sam never says how he wants it cutting, and they generally do a good job.

This time the language barrier has meant that he has a rather shorter 'do' than usual. As Sam puts it, 'He just kept going round and round. It seemed best to let him get on with it.'

He looks about 12.

## 11 September

Clive really earns his keep today by making not one, but two date and walnut loaves. We have a new oven and after years of cooking more by luck than judgement, this one has a very complicated and to me unnecessary combination of knobs and settings. However, even I must admit that there is something very satisfying about watching through that glass door as cake batter turn into actual cake.

While the loaves are baking, he turns his attention to processing about ten pounds of beetroot, a mountain of runner beans and yet more courgettes, all destined for the freezer. This most recent haul of veg from the plot also included a few sad-looking parsnips, which were barely worth picking and will make scant difference to a stock pot. I'm moved to take a picture of one with a 1p piece for scale and stick it on Facebook. It is rather galling that while some of my more literary contributions barely get noticed, this frivolous offering receives more Likes, Shares and Comments than anything I have ever posted. People are strange.

## 12 September
It's Wednesday, which, yes, means a trip to B&Q. There's nothing Clive particularly wants, but he sets off to have a look just in case he thinks of something he needs. He comes back with a piece of guttering. One of the benefits of living with a retired man is that he now has time to do all those little running repairs that have needed doing for donkey's years.

I am forced to eat my words when Sports Direct changes the trainers without any fuss.

This afternoon I am told by a car insurance company that I don't qualify for a discount on my premium because I work in publishing, which is classed as a risky profession. Given that I spend most of my time sitting still, I can only wonder what might be consider a safe profession.

## 13 September
Further investigations into the wonderful world of U3A have resulted in Clive planning to go to a meeting next Tuesday, a decision spurred on by the discovery that

there is a golf group that meets every Friday. This afternoon he goes off for a round with his regular partner. Meanwhile I panic about an impending ukulele performance on Saturday. My fingers seem to have forgotten where the notes are.

## 14 September

We have a run up the M1 to see Mum, ahead of her birthday tomorrow: 89! She is in fine fettle, busy organising a concert to commemorate the end of the First World War, and sitting on a committee choosing pieces for her writing group's anthology. My brother Neil pops in at lunchtime with an update on his mother-in-law's precarious health.

On the way home the motorway is at a standstill going north and we are glad we are going the other way. We pass a lorry that proclaims it is carrying 'mixed grill freight'. This is either a truck full of bacon and chops, or, more likely, it means that the driver will carry anything if the price is right. I decide *Mixed Grill* will make an excellent title for a short story collection.

## 15 September

It's Strum Like A Pirate Day and I wake up with a sore throat. Suitably dosed up, I head off to the Yards Bar with my uke under my arm and my skull-and-crossbones bandana in place and, despite feeling like death warmed up, manage to have a pretty good time.

Clive dutifully stands in the crowd and Sam also pops in for an hour. Joe is excused because he is at work.

## 16 September
While I sit on the sofa coughing and blowing my nose, Clive performs more miracles in the kitchen. Today he produces Golden Syrup Cake, which is sublime. The best nurse is one who keeps you topped up with carbs.

## 17 September
The morning is spent bottling beer, a very messy process that needs four hands. I hold the bottles while Clive rams on the tops with a device that looks like something from the London Dungeon. About one top in five needs serious persuading, so what should be a straightforward job ends up causing serious angst. At least none of the bottles breaks this time.

After lunch, while I try to do a bit of work through a haze of paracetamol and cough medicine, Clive spends all afternoon up at the allotment. Things are winding down, but there is still work to be done before the end of the season. As well as picking yet more beans and courgettes, he dismantles the sweetcorn. Next will be digging up the rest of the potatoes to be brought home, washed and bagged in the shed. The squashes will be stored in the spare bedroom (obviously). There are a few leeks to be tended, but confidence is not high.

## 18 September

Mostly to stop me nagging, I suspect, Clive trots along to a U3A meeting this afternoon. He isn't impressed. Although the person on the door recognises his name from his email to her a couple of days ago, the so-called greeter to whom he is directed simply tells him to get himself a cup of tea and sit down. Oh, and to buy a raffle ticket. He tells me he shuffled about for a bit, then did as he was told and sat in splendid isolation. Nobody spoke to him.

He takes out his frustrations by mowing the lawn with great gusto.

## 19 September

Golf today and on his return Clive declares he has had the best round ever, playing well below his handicap and giving his mate a good whipping in the process. Not that he's gloating.

In the evening, and notwithstanding the disdain of the U3A yesterday, Clive sallies forth on his own to a talk at the local art gallery. The topic is archaeology, in which subject he has an O-level. He comes home having spoken to strangers and won a raffle prize, a strange pottery bird feeder that is itself shaped like a bird. Still, a prize is a prize, and Clive declares that today has been a good day.

## 20 September

The spare part for the scarifier has finally arrived, so with the aid of three hammers and a bit of swearing it is installed and the lawn now looks well and truly scarified, not to mention scared.

Two magpies descend in the garden, strutting around like barristers with their arms tucked behind them. The doves are not impressed and divebomb the magpies who give them a look of scorn before flying off. Moments later they are back and there is another brief dogfight before an uneasy truce is reached. The doves sit on the fence and watch, while the magpies scour the lawn for tasty morsels. Clearly the scarifier has unearthed something worth pursuing.

In due course the magpies notice the new bird feeder hanging from the shed. They look at it, then at each other as they consider whether it is worth the effort. Eventually one of them launches at it, but its slippery finish offers little purchase and bird and feeder are left swinging violently in the breeze.

## 21 September

The day passes quickly enough with work for me and chores for him. Then it's off to Kettering Arts Centre. The centre is actually St Andrew's Church: not a disused church, but an actual, working church, complete with a licensed bar in one corner. Every month it plays host to the Rolling in the Aisles Comedy Club (see what they did there?). The vicar Nick is the club's MC and he's very good at it.

Tonight, though, is a special night, because Nish Kumar is on. Yes, him off the telly. Nick must have friends in high places (ahem), because over the years we've had some really big names: Marcus Brigstocke, Milton Jones, Ramesh Ranganathan and Jack Dee, not to mention Kettering's own James Acaster.

We meet one of Clive's former workmates there, accompanied by his daughter. It's not long before Clive and Richard are talking about work and Clive is soon up to speed on the gossip at the old place: who's still there, who's left, who's up to no good. As time passes and the beer flows, I hear Clive holding forth about how great it is to be retired and offering to take a look at Richard's pension plan for him.

## 22 September
I escape to a yoga workshop, leaving Clive making plans for the day. The weather isn't very promising, but he reckons there are jobs to be done. I'm not surprised to find on my return that he has done a lot of planning, but not much of anything else. Mind you, I can't say I blame him. At the workshop we are asked to think about what might be stopping us from being content. To my surprise, the thought arises that I am envious of Clive's new station. His guilt-free day spent in contemplation and comfy tracksuit bottoms only serves to highlight my small-mindedness.

## 23 September

For the second time in a week, we watch *The Greatest Showman*. By his own admission, Clive has a bit of a weakness for a soppy film (*Love Actually*, *Notting Hill* – you get the idea), but I'm surprised he likes this one, given that it's a musical. The very thought of *Les Misérables* can send him running to the hills, though he has been known to sit through *Chicago*. All those women in stockings, I suspect.

Once the film has finished, we flick around the channels for a few idle moments and happen upon an episode of *One Foot In The Grave*. Long-suffering wife Margaret has lost her job and is anxious that she will end up like her retired and grumpy husband Victor, 'struggling to fill up my days with mad cookery recipes and playing with dolls'. We avoid each other's eye.

## 24 September

Today's mystery object: a sunhat full of pebbles. Unable to see why I think this is a tad odd, Clive patiently explains that an ongoing task at the allotment is to clear the beds of stones. What better way to do this than to bring them home to put in his tumbler? It crosses my mind to suggest that he could have put them in a plant pot, but I decide not to pursue this.

He's also got a touch of tool envy. A chap on a neighbouring plot has treated himself to an automatic spade. I think this is a joke, so I Google it, and sure enough it's a real thing. Apparently, you can shift twice as much soil than with a conventional spade and without the backache. You stick the spade spit in the ground, pull back on the handles and a large spring at the base of the device throws the soil forward and turns it over. The model I looked at has 'a lovely sharp edge, galvanised fixings and comfy-grip PVC handles'. Wow.

## 25 September

A planned expedition to Staffordshire is blessed with glorious autumn sunshine. We are off to The Black Lion in Consall, which is the sort of pub you can only reach by going to the end of the world and on a bit. It's deep in the countryside, nestling between a canal and a preserved railway line. Our companions are my mum and her friend Sir Malcolm (yes, another Malcolm), a baronet and a gent in so many ways, but whose politics and fruity language often make me wince. He is, as always, lively company.

We overhear the barmaid on the phone to the authorities:

'A man has been spotted by one of our customers. He was walking through the country park wearing nothing but a rucksack.'

Thinking we might have misheard we call her over, but we are right. There is indeed a naked rambler in the vicinity.

The barmaid is rueful: 'I wish I could say it's the first time this has happened.'

(Postscript: I write up this visit and enter it into a travel writing competition, and am rewarded with £50.)

## 26 September

Oh no! B&Q is restricting its Diamond Club discount to certain gardening items! We may have to consider our position. Fortunately, sharp sand still qualifies, so the challenge of resurrecting the lawn continues.

Our neighbour has a new toy: a serious-looking chainsaw. Clive whimpers with envy. This chap has recently redesigned his garden in the course of which project he has dug up his lawn and replaced it with gravel chippings and a lovely central paved area. It looks very smart. This means that he no longer needs his mower, which has gone to one of his sons, or his spreader, a sort of fancy bucket on wheels that is used to dispense seed, fertiliser and whatever else the grass needs. He trades this device with Clive in return for a trug-load of onions and garlic from our allotment. Our neighbour has a pizza oven, so both men are happy with the barter.

## 27 September

I am grumpy today. I have no work deadline and flop about aimlessly while Clive is busy doing all sorts of things. This is exactly the opposite of what I was expecting. I encouraged Clive to retire, so why am I envious of his new status? I am ashamed of myself.

Clive wisely ignores my mardiness and ploughs on with the task of aerating the lawn with a fork. There is a moment of excitement when he discovers a layer of rock less than a tine's length beneath the surface. We dig a hole and discover a lump of something that could be builder's rubble or, just possibly, something more interesting. Clive chips off a bit and has a closer look at it under his geology lens. Is it concrete? We fill in the hole, but are intrigued. Perhaps we'll try to find out what was on the plot before our house was built.

## 28 September

I'm still a bit grumpy, but manage to keep myself together, and our evening's entertainment improves my mood no end. We go to the Arts Centre to see Colin Cloud – Forensic Mind-Reader, a sort of Derren Brown turn who has been on *America's Got Talent*, *The Royal Variety Show* and, to top it all, on the *Good Morning* sofa with Phil and Holly. There can surely be no greater recommendation.

Two seats have been reserved on the front row for a couple who fail to turn up, so Becky, who runs the centre with Nick, invites us to move forwards. This is risky, given the likelihood of audience participation, but in the event our only involvement is when Clive has to place his fingers on Colin's eyes to stop him peeping. It is a very clever show and, while we know it is all trickery, it is nonetheless jaw-droppingly mysterious. We come home saying, 'What just happened?'

## 29 September

We go into town to see my friend Adrian, who is doing a book signing, and to do a few amiable tasks. We call in at the museum to see the new 'Local Treasures' exhibition, which comprises artefacts local to Kettering that are part of the British Museum's collection. It's fascinating stuff. What strikes us is what presence of mind people have when they discover what to the untutored eye looks like a bit of scrap metal or a broken plate. Who knows what treasures I've discarded over the years.

There is a sticky moment in Superdrug when we decide the best way to choose shower gel is take off the top and have a sniff. For some reason, Clive decides you can't do this without squeezing the bottle, and we both end up covered in cherry-and-almond-flavoured bubble mix. You can't take us anywhere.

## 30 September

We take advantage of a bright, mild morning to go for a walk on one our regular routes. It's just under three miles, but every little helps, as the old lady said as she peed in the sea. We set off on pavements through a housing estate, but then cut in through a patch of council-owned grass where boys of all ages are playing Sunday League football. There is, inevitably, a fat dad on the touchline shouting the odds, convinced that he knows more about the rules than the ref and the linesmen.

We cut into the fields and walk across the Duke of Buccleuch's fields to the woodlands that come out by the allotment, taking a detour to pick what I hope is finally the last of the courgettes. Then it's home via the Co-op for a pint of milk and a determination not to buy a Danish pastry to go with our coffee.

There are calories aplenty later in the day when we celebrate a friend's birthday with that most English of occasions, afternoon tea. It is lovely, and we both decide that the diet can wait, because there are scones and cream tartlets on offer.

# OCTOBER

## 1 October
We go to PMT Northampton Music Shop to pick up something for Joe's birthday. This is a wonderful Aladdin's Cave of a place, two floors of guitars, drums, leads, amps and other performance-related gear. Clive looks longingly at a 12-string hanging on the wall underneath a stern sign warning 'Do Not Touch

Without Permission From The Staff'. I lure him away with the promise of lunch.

Back home, he sets about cooking a joint of pork for him and Sam to share later, during the course of which he embarks on the most flamboyant sneezing fit. He sneezes 16 times in a row with increasing vigour and expends so much energy that it leaves him quite breathless. I laugh.

## 2 October

Yesterday, Clive had said there have so far only been a couple of days when he's felt a bit bored. Today, however, we wake to grey skies and no plan. There will be many more of these days as the weather draws in, so it is becoming urgent to find something he can do over winter or he will drive me crazy. Today, however, Paul comes to the rescue with the offer of a game of golf this afternoon. Naturally, Clive comes home the victor.

## 3 October

There is a note on today's page in my diary, in my handwriting. It says 'MELTING' and I have no idea what this means. Best guess is that I got distracted trying to write 'Melanie's birthday', but that seems a long shot.

## 4 October

Clive has a quiet day during which nothing of note occurs. I go off to teach yoga in a nearby village and get tangled up with toffs and hounds preparing to go off hunting. I wait politely while they trot and scamper past me, with their noses in the air. They do not even register that I am there.

## 5 October

Joe's birthday today and he, Caitlin, Sam and Clive are off to Alton Towers to celebrate. As with their trip to Thorpe Park earlier this year, it goes without saying that I stay at home. They return tired but happy. My day is enlivened by a visit from Sir Malcolm. We put the world to rights over a cuppa and to the surprise of both of us find some common political ground.

## 6 October

Clive earns many Brownie points today. It is the day of a big charity concert for our ukulele group and choir. A lot of hard work has gone on behind the scenes by those few of us who like to get involved. It's amazing how interesting the floor becomes for some people when the call goes out for volunteers. Anyway, Clive goes above and beyond by setting out 150 chairs, taking tickets on the door, acting as bouncer (you'd be surprised!), then packing away the chairs again at the end. The concert is a huge success and we raise about £800 to be divided between Cransley Hospice and Headway East Northants, which cares for brain-injured adults and their families and carers.

Neither of us has eaten much all day, so at half ten we are chowing down on pizza and drinking homebrew, living the dream.

**7 October**

More celebrations for Joe's birthday and the family come over for afternoon tea. Clive gets in a panic over his buttercream, but in the event the lemon cake he produces for the occasion is absolutely delicious. This is why I married him.

*Doctor Who* is back on TV with Jodie Whittaker in the title role. The opening episode is not without its flaws – clearly someone has been through the *Diversity Handbook* with a fine-tooth comb – and Bradley Walsh needs to up his game, but overall we are pleased. It has a gentler feel than the previous season and we are optimistic that the franchise will survive not only the gender switch, but also the move to Sunday evenings. Like any of this matters in the grand scheme of things.

**8 October**

I have lots of work on this week and get up extra early to get a head start. At 8.20 I get a request to cover a yoga class at 9. Grateful that I had an early breakfast, I set off.

Clive decides to have a 'rest day' and after a little gentle pottering settles himself down in front of Amazon Prime. While browsing we discover that the American version of *The Office* is back on, so I treat myself to an episode while I have a spot of lunch, then a couple more in the evening. That's the trouble with streamed box sets; you only get a few seconds to decide whether or not to watch another episode and by the time you've concluded that you've already sat for long enough another one has started and, well, it would be churlish not to watch it. We may be addicts.

**9 October**
After a slow start, which included returning to bed after breakfast to read another chapter of his book, Clive draws himself up a list of jobs, the first of which it to pop down to the Co-op for the ingredients to make some mackerel pâté. Unfortunately he doesn't take any money with him, so falls at the first fence. He sets off instead to have a haircut and returns a short time later looking quite splendid. He has also brought the cooking ingredients and the results are worth the wait.

The *Strictly Curse* seems have struck again. Poor old Seann Walsh and his dance partner Katya Jones have been caught having a bit of a drunken snog and the sky has fallen in on them. Social media are overjoyed.

**10 October**
We switched on the heating on Sunday, but it's gone off again because today the temperature is back up to 22°C. What's going on? The fine weather tempts Clive and his chums out to Priors Hall for a round of golf, and I can't say I blame him.

First, though, the postman comes to the door with a box slightly bigger all round than a sheet of A4 and nearly 3 inches deep. It contains a single £2 coin. Not just any old coin, mind you; this one is solid silver and is the latest of the Queen's Beasts that Clive is collecting. This one is the Falcon of the Plantagenets and goes with the Lion of England, the Unicorn of Scotland (yes, really), the Red Dragon of Wales and the Black Bull of Clarence.

'Lovely,' I say. 'Is that the last one in the set?'

It seems not. Still to come is a white lion, a yale (which in case you're wondering is a bit like a horse, but has tusks, horns and an elephant's tail), a white greyhound, a white horse and a griffin.

## 11 October

I have lunch with a friend today who asks me, 'How's it going with the new normal, then?'

I find myself confessing that any problems are of my own making. Clive is settling down nicely into a new routine, but I'm struggling a bit, if I'm honest. I'm reluctant to let go of the household chores (because Clive doesn't do them right – that is to say, not like I do them), but I moan if I have to do them myself. There's no pleasing some people.

## 12 October

Justin the plumber comes round to take a look at a few jobs that are beyond our modest skills. When it comes to pipes and water, it's not worth taking any chances and we have called on Justin many a time. He is what you might call a Diamond Geezer, a man who works with great intensity and enthusiasm and the most extraordinary attention to detail. Not for the first time we wonder where his energy comes from, because he's as thin as one of the drainpipes he manoeuvres into place outside our kitchen window, and from what he tells us about his work-hard-play-hard life he can't have time to sleep. He bounces in and gets straight to business, no chat and no pre-work cuppa. We have recommended him to several friends and he has never let down either them or us. As I type this, he is outside my office window working miracles with our guttering. Everyone needs a Justin in their life.

In other news, Princess Eugenie has married her beau Jack Brooksbank today, an occasion that nearly passed me by. She is, of course, only ninth in line to the throne, which makes her virtually a commoner, but she looks lovely, despite the best efforts of Storm Callum to dislodge the finery of the wedding guests. At least it's taken our minds off Brexit, and Seann and Katya must be glad not to be top of the 'trending' list for a while. Let it go, people!

**13 October**
I have the potential to be grumpy today, feeling curiously dissatisfied with everything, without any justification whatsoever. Clive, adept at spotting the

signs, takes me for a walk. Much cheered, I then sit in the garden and read in the autumn sunshine. It really is ridiculously warm.

In the evening we go to the Arts Centre to see Juliette Burton's show, 'The Butterfly Effect', which evolved from her experiences with just about every mental illness you've ever heard of. Not on the face of it a good basis for a comedy show, but it was very funny, while also being thought-provoking. A woman a few seats away was in tears at one point.

The premise was to consider whether small, random acts of kindness can change the world. Based on this show I'd say yes. We were all invited to write down a suggestion for such an act and put it in a bowl for distribution to the audience of a future show. I wrote 'Leave a bunch of flowers on your neighbour's doorstep.' We were all given a suggestion from a previous show and mine was 'Smile and chat with someone you don't know.' Naturally I turned to the person next to me on the front row, who turned out to be a first-timer at the venue. The suggestion for Clive was to lead a standing ovation at a comedy show, which proved easy to do tonight.

Given the shaky start my day had, this is a very pleasing end.

## 14 October

It's hammering down with rain today as the tail end of Storm Callum passes over. We decide to tackle the spare bedroom, which has become a dumping ground for things that need somewhere to go 'just for now'. It is quite cathartic to come downstairs with bags of rubbish. We also reveal several items that might be worth a punt on eBay, so Clive sets to with his camera while I oversee the writing of the blurb. By bedtime we have already received a couple of bids, which is encouraging.

In the evening, Clive, Sam, Joe and Caitlin go to the Lighthouse Theatre here in town to see Rich Hall. I don't go, because I thought I would be working. They have a splendid time without me (again).

## 15 October

It's still raining, so Clive puts on his brewer's apron and gets to work. My morning is pleasantly interrupted several times with the invitation to have a little taste of blackcurrant wine as he racks off the demijohns that were in the spare bedroom.

Then he starts to make the SMaSH brew for which he bought the necessary back in August. I happen to be in the kitchen just when the sparge bag threatens to overflow, so I'm called on to lend a hand. What an honour! He is using the same ingredients as last time (Maris Otter barley and East Kent Gold hops), but making a bigger batch. At the start of the process the kitchen smells rather like he's just strawed down a cowshed, but gradually the aroma changes to something altogether more appealing. The beer should be ready in time for Christmas.

## 16 October

We had an interesting conversation the other night about the stock market. Apparently there's been a bit of a slump that hasn't been reported in the mainstream media, though no doubt it's been in the *Financial Times*. This means that £7,000 has been wiped off our total pot, which sounds awful to me, but Clive is sanguine about it. These things happen, apparently, and all it means is that our fund is now back down to where it was six months ago. I don't understand such things, but I'm happy to trust him.

Today, while we are celebrating, if that's the word, the news that the Duke and Duchess of Sussex (aka Harry and Meghan) are expecting their first child, news of the fracking in Lancashire goes unreported. On Monday we were all horrified that it was due to begin again, but today the story has mysteriously disappeared from the BBC News webpages. I'm not a conspiracy theorist, but it does make me wonder.

Also on the baby news front, Pippa Middleton has produced a child. Wow.

## 17 October

There might be a problem with the SMaSH brew! It should by now be bubbling away like a good 'un, but it is worryingly quiet. We take the lid off the fermentation bucket to investigate. There is a layer of something brown on the top, which we hope is a good sign, but there's not a lot of action. Clive gives it a good whipping with a spatula, adds more yeast, tapes a heat belt to the side, wraps the whole thing in a sleeping-bag and puts it back under the stairs. We cross our fingers.

## 18 October

There are signs of life in the beer, but it still doesn't look quite right. Could we be on the brink of our first brewing disaster?

In the evening we go to the Derngate to see Ross Noble. We take Sam, Joe and Caitlin, and we all laugh like drains for the whole show. Having said that, I do put my fingers in my ears and shut my eyes tight while he did several minutes about vomit, a topic I never find remotely amusing.

## 19 October

I take a day off, and after a little gentle pottering we head into town to the art gallery, where there is a free talk on 'Treasures in Northamptonshire', thus giving further proof of our middle class-ness.

It is a warm day, the room is a bit stuffy and the lights are dimmed so we can see the screen properly. We aren't surprised, then, when an elderly lady a couple of rows in front of us appears to nod off about halfway through. She leans on the shoulder of the woman to her left, who pushes her back over to the right, where she rests on the shoulder of a man. This couple are definitely with the old lady, perhaps her son and daughter-in-law.

Anyway, the old lady slumps right down in her seat and the man tries to rouse her by shaking her arm. Then he puts his hand around the back of her neck and hoicks her upright, rather like a cat might gather up a kitten. The lady stays in place for a few seconds, but then slumps back on to his shoulder. This makes us smile at first; but then we start to wonder if perhaps something is amiss, and yet neither of the chaperones seems unduly concerned and they keep their attention firmly on the speaker.

It is only at the end, when the lights come back on, that it becomes clear the lady is not asleep. At best she has passed out. (Clive assures me she is still breathing, but I'm not convinced. I think he is sparing my feelings. When I was in hospital having one of our boys, he told me that the trolleys that I now realise actually contained bodies were laundry carts.) Very discreetly, gallery staff ask us to clear the room as the lady is moved to the floor. As we leave, we hear an ambulance approaching.

We wonder about the conversation that had taken place before she set off on what might well have been her last trip out. Did she want to go to the talk? Did she feel unwell at home, but didn't want to say for fear of upsetting her well-meaning family? Did she realise she was drifting while she sat listening to the talk? Why didn't the man grasp that she wasn't just asleep? It was all rather sobering.

## 20 October

Another glorious autumn day dawns and, because we had a day off yesterday, today – Saturday – feels like an extra day, which is lovely.

Our friend Kezzabelle is having a book launch for her latest poetry collection, so we go down to the Yards Bar to support her and have a couple of pints. There are lots of people there we know and we have a splendid time. Walking home at about 10pm, we meet lots of bright young things walking the other way, just setting out for their evening's fun and to my mind woefully underdressed. God, we're old.

## 21 October

It's lovely spending all this time together, but we're starting to get on each other's nerves, so it's as well that Clive goes off to play a round of golf. I stay at home to potter and read, treating myself to a walk round the park. I don't speak to anyone all day, which is perfect. That evening we veg out on the sofa, harmony restored by a day apart.

## 22 October

It's half-term and some of my friends are teachers, so I skive off to have coffee with them and put the world to rights. Clive has made some biscuits for me to take, which one of my friends declares are as good as Marks and Spencer's. Praise indeed! The secret is meticulous weighing. Not content with making sure there is the correct quantity of each ingredient, he then weighs each individual ball of dough so that the finished biscuits are all exactly the same size. I would have done it by eye, which is why I'm not very good at making biscuits.

While I'm out, Clive decides the time has come to fix the hall. We had a leaky shower a while ago and there is an unsightly stain where the water came through. If I were in charge, I'd take off the minimum of damaged paper and bodge it. Fortunately, Clive is more scrupulous and tackles the job with the same precision as his baking, which is why he is so much better at decorating that I am.

## 23 October

Today I have two men at work in the house, each equipped with his own set of dust sheets and proving his worth not just at the task in hand, but also at the hoovering round afterwards. Clive continues to work miracles in the hallway. The curious thing is that having stripped away some of the old ceiling paper the new pieces, which definitely came from the same roll, are slightly narrower. How can this be?

Meanwhile, a young man called James has been called to fix the fire, again. It has one of those irritating faults that only shows itself once James has gone home. Again I ask, how can this be?

86

## 24 October

I am up against a work deadline today, so Clive keeps himself occupied and well out of my way. Joe pops round for some drums, but that is the only event of note all day.

## 25 October

My morning yoga class is cancelled, which means I'm able to plough on towards my deadline. James arrives as promised and declares there is nothing wrong with our fire. Nevertheless he takes it all to pieces, fiddles with the thermocouple, then puts it all together. He switches the fire on and it lights first time. He stays for 20 minutes waiting for it to go out, but it burns steadily. This should be pleasing, but for some reason we are both slightly disappointed. James must think we are making it up.

## 26 October

We are not the sort of couple who argues. That is to say, I am, but Clive rarely fights back. Today, though, it is he who fires the first shot and we have a 'discussion' about who is the more irritating, him or me. What we should have done is resolved to spend the day apart. Instead, with my birthday looming, we decide to go shopping for boots for me.

I am not a good clothes shopper. It agitates me beyond all reason and footwear is particularly challenging, because I have stupidly small feet. Taking courage in both hands, we venture to the factory shop that has an overwhelming range of stock. We browse and I see a couple that take my fancy, but I can't see my size. However, there are signs everywhere that tell me if that is the case all I have to do is ask. Two women members of staff are deep in conversation but I manage to attract their attention by waving and jumping up and down shouting 'Coo-ee!'

I brandish a boot in each hand: 'Do you have either of these in a size three, please?'

'If it's not out, we don't have it. You could try the children's section.'

With that, they return to their conversation. I am speechless with rage. I'm tempted to say, 'Ok, let's run that scene again. I'll ask for a size three and you will say, "Let me check for you. No, I'm sorry. Is there anything else you like the look of that we might have in your size? No? OK, well some of the children's range goes up to size four so there might be something there. Let me show you where it is. Still no good? I'm sorry we couldn't help you today and I hope you find something somewhere else."'

My day is ruined and I sulk all afternoon. Clive spends the day wearing his best kid gloves.

## 27 October

While I am out all day at the Moulton Literary Festival, networking, presenting and trying to sell books, Clive performs a miracle with the hoover and a duster. My brother Tim comes down for the evening and we all go to Rolling in the Aisles Comedy Club. There are three good acts this evening, the first of whom, Paul Pirie, takes great pleasure in insulting individual audience members. My friend gets called Noodle Head, Clive is labelled a silver fox, and I am told I have Lego hair. Oh, how I laughed.

## 28 October

After a busy week and several late nights I have a lazy day, enhanced by an extra hour in bed as the clocks go back. Clive spends the whole day in the kitchen, baking, and produces a lemon meringue pie of such height that it almost makes me want to share a picture of it online. Almost, but not quite, because I'm not an idiot.

We eventually switch on the TV, learning that yesterday evening the owner of Leicester City FC died when his helicopter crashed outside the stadium. Billionaire Vichai Srivaddhanaprabha, two members of his staff, the pilot and a passenger were killed when the aircraft spiralled out of control and crashed in a fireball on to a disused car park. He was clearly a very popular man, not just with the club but also the city itself, and this is sad news for all involved. However, this is the first item on the main evening news, taking precedence over the story that also on Saturday 11 people were shot dead in a Pittsburgh synagogue during a child's naming ceremony. One of the victims is a 97-year-old man who survived the Holocaust. It's a strange world.

## 29 October

Another year older. This time it is an unspeakable prime number, so Clive kindly suggests it will be a 'prime year'. It might be my birthday, but there is still work to be done. I'm sitting at my computer, but can hear the food mixer going, which is encouraging. Then Clive comes into the office, rummages in his desk and retrieves a pair of pliers. I've been known to take a chisel to my pastry, but I'm disconcerted as to why he should resort to such desperate measures. He returns the tool a few minutes later and says simply, 'Sorted.' I decide it's best not to ask.

## 30 October

After a lovely extended birthday weekend, it's back to work today. I spend the day in splendid isolation because Clive takes himself off to the allotment. I move a mountain of paper and feel very pleased with myself. Clive comes home six hours later having dug himself to a standstill. There are a few carrots and leeks to show for it, and a pair of aching buttocks.

## 31 October

Despite his grumbling glutes, Clive goes off to the plot again. There is still plenty to do, even though it is now officially the 'back end' of the year. On his return, as he tells me what he's achieved he announces he's cleared 240 stones from the soil. When I ask how he knows this, he says he counted them out into batches of ten. Makes sense, I suppose.

Amongst the challenges I face today is a three-mile car trip that takes me 90 minutes. I'm on my way to see a new client and fear he will think me terribly unprofessional. As it turns out, he has also been held captive by the traffic and is understanding. I get the job.

# NOVEMBER

## 1 November

Trouble in the brew house. There is definitely something wrong with the SMaSH brew. It should have been bottled today, but it has a funny taste. I can't decide if it's bleach or ammonia. What is clear is that if it were a urine sample, the vet would definitely declare the horse unfit for work. Even Clive is forced to admit it's not right. He decants a sample and takes it up to the Copper Kettle for a diagnosis. Bad news: the whole lot is tainted by something, probably caused by overheating at some point. The drinking world's loss is the compost heap's gain.

## 2 November
Old friends come to lunch. I've known Jenny since we were five years old. While she and I settle down to catch up on all the gossip, Clive and her husband Ian disappear to inspect the brewing empire and the ripening harvest of squashes reclining in the spare bedroom. It's either that, or they're playing with the Lego we still have, despite us not having any small children any more.

## 3 November
Having taken off most of yesterday, I decide to do some work, even though it's Saturday. It's a lovely day, though, so I decide I can justify a walk into town. I wish I hadn't. I don't see anyone I know and there are so many empty shops interspersed among the vaping emporiums and cafés that the whole experience is quite dispiriting. I return to the comfort of my computer. Meanwhile, Clive goes to the plot and comes home smelling of bonfires and fresh air.

In the evening we go to an interactive drama about austerity. Not many laughs in it, as you might imagine, but it is a thought-provoking performance.

**4 November**

I still haven't caught up from Friday, so I do a bit of editing this morning, then we both potter about and fill the day in individual pursuits. This is definitely the harmonious way forward.

**5 November**

We declare that Monday is the new Saturday, and skive off to Northampton. It is so mild today that we sit outside for coffee and Danish at the Bistro at All Saints Church. It is a successful trip; I buy not one but two pairs of boots without having a tantrum.

Following our drink, Clive follows the older gentleman's maxim of one pee per pint or part thereof and disappears to the Gents. He returns with a suspicious-looking damp patch on the front of his trousers, which he attributes to an overenthusiastic tap.

'S'pose this will end up on your blog,' he grumbles. 'I don't mind, if you think it will raise a laugh.' He doesn't yet know about this diary.

**6 November**

A morose Joe turns up on the doorstep. He got up to discover that some joker had wrenched one of his wiper blades off, not the rubber bit, but the whole thing, right from the base. It must have taken some force to do. Obviously, he can't drive it in the rain – it *would* be the driver's side – so he's going to need a chauffeur for the next couple of days. That's what dads are for, especially retired dads. It's going to cost £90 to fix, and he's just paid his insurance, and his car tax is due at the end of the month. Heigh-ho.

**7 November**
Clive girds his loins to have another go at a SMaSH brew. Never needing any excuse to buy a new gadget, he is now the proud owner of a digital scale that will enable him to weigh a single gram of yeast, which he tells me is a good thing. Certainly the smell coming from the kitchen is promising.

**8 November**
The apple wine that sits in bottles in the corner of my office, pending removal upstairs, has started exploding. Well, not exploding in the sense that it is showering glass and juice all over everything, but more a gentle chorus of pops and bangs as the corks fly out. This is why the bottles don't go straight into storage, of course, just in case the wine is still 'working'. Nevertheless it's quite disconcerting to be typing away in stillness and then to have something take a shot at me.

I point this out to Clive, but he just says, 'Don't worry, it's fine.'

Oh, that's all right, then.

**9 November**
I skive off again so that we can go to visit Lyveden Manor, on the same site as Lyveden New Bield, but

only recently acquired by the National Trust. The purpose of the visit today is to have a sneak peek behind the scenes to see what the Trust has in mind for it. We have a lovely time and are very impressed at what we see. Of course, no visit to an NT property is complete without a trip to the tea shop, which is where we inevitably end up. The place is a sea of grey hair and bald heads. The cheese scones are, as always, fabulous.

## 10 November

My lazy week catches up with me and I have to spend the day working, even though it's Saturday. I'm not sure what Clive does, but he's quiet, so I leave well alone. The evening takes us to friend Debs' house for an early supper and then we go to the theatre – or was it the cinema? It was a live streaming of the National Theatre's production of Alan Bennett's new play *Alleluia!* You had me at Alan.

Once again, we are surrounded by grey hair. It's easy to forget that we are well on the way to joining that gang.

## 11 November

Neither of us generally pays much heed to Remembrance Sunday beyond observing the two minutes' silence, but this year we watch the ceremony at the Cenotaph in London because it's 100 years since the end of the First World War. It is very moving.

I have been trying to find out what my maternal grandfather did during the war, but it's proving quite challenging, even though he had an unusual name. He was Joseph Primrose Pattinson, named for the Primrose League, which was founded in 1883 to promote Conservatism in Britain. I shall push on. Meanwhile, a cousin posts on Facebook that my other grandfather (my dad and this cousin's mother were siblings) found an ivory crucifix on a battlefield in France. She also tells me he was a PoW. Why didn't I know this?

**12 November**
With a little encouragement, Clive has renewed his acquaintance with the OU Geology Society. He studied natural sciences with the university and has been persuaded to get involved with something called RIGS. I don't know what this stands for, but it's to do with visiting geological sites throughout the county to see if they are still accessible and to record what there is to see and what state they're in.

He comes back from his first meeting enthused at the thought of grubbing about in the undergrowth looking for ironstone deposits, but slightly frustrated at the vagueness of his potential colleagues in this project. It is, I suppose, inevitable that people slow down once released from the yoke of employment, but why do so many seem to switch off their brains and come to a virtual standstill? I shall not let this happen to Clive, even if he wants it to.

## 13 November

The wine is still popping its corks and I am starting to get annoyed. To pacify me, Clive breaks off from cleaning out the fish tank to take all the corks out to release the build-up. I'm more concerned about the bottles with screw tops, so with a patient sigh he takes these off, too, and replaces them. It must be such a trial to live with me.

## 14 November

Another day, another bed dug over. Clive comes back from the allotment with some feeble-looking leeks that will nonetheless be a welcome addition to the soup later. Where would we be without soup? He looks so knackered I wonder if he might have overdone it a bit, but he assures me he's fine.

## 15 November

Whether it was the indigestion that kept waking him in the night or he actually did do too much yesterday I couldn't say, but Clive spends most of the day lolling about. I pull on my finest martyr pants and set about my work with an inflated sense of my own importance.

Also today, my new phone arrived. Yes, against my better judgement I have bought a smartphone. This means that I shall now be carrying my work contacts with me everywhere I go, which does not please me. However, there are times when I've wanted to post something work related when I've been out and about –

I gave a talk to the WI recently, for instance, and it might have been useful to be able to do a 'Look where I am post' – and I'm sure I'll make good use of the camera function, if only to take photos of stupid people parking. However, it nearly goes in the bin this afternoon when it keeps offering me suggestions for downloading this or setting up that. Clive thinks I'm a Luddite; I call him Inspector Gadget.

## 16 November

This is better. I have cause to go out this morning and when I return Clive is halfway through cleaning the house, top to bottom. Then he goes to Sainsbury's and, with the attention to detail that only a scientist would apply to the task, manages to spend just over the threshold to make maximum use of the vouchers the supermarket has sent us. They must hate people like us, but not as much as the Halifax, which several years ago gave us a generous cashback credit card on which we have never paid a single penny of interest, but have accrued hundreds of what can only be described as free pounds. Sticking it to the man.

To crown an already satisfactory day, Clive goes out into the dismal evening and returns with fish and chips. All that remains is to sink into the sofa to watch the Children in Need malarkey.

By the way, the Brexit fiasco continues. Theresa May is likely to be facing a vote of no confidence before the weekend is out. Her cabinet is deserting her and she looks on the verge of tears every time she appears on the news. I am choosing not to go into details here, because it's all just too awful to contemplate.

## 17 November

After a busy week, I force myself to take it easy today; we both do. We stroll around a Christmas fair at Wicksteed Park and come back with a couple of presents, some chutney and having ordered a bespoke bird table. Not quite sure how that last thing happened.

The evening brings a night of comedy at the Arts Centre, courtesy of Alfie Moore, a police officer turned comic whom we award 7 out of 10. It's not his fault, but the people he chooses for a little audience participation turn out to be worse than useless. One woman, chosen to be the (pretend) murderer, is given an inflatable baseball bat to use as a weapon. When invited to clout the victim over the head, she declines and merely gives him a gentle tap that wouldn't have disturbed a gnat, never mind felled a six-foot villain. What should have been a glorious comedy moment turned into an embarrassment.

## 18 November

Capitalising on Monday's rejuvenation of Clive's geological leanings, we set off to explore one of the sites on the RIGS list. We can't believe that there is a nature reserve we've never heard off only five miles from our house, but it turns out there is. I enjoy the walk in the sunshine, while Clive, in his element, disappears into the undergrowth with his hand lens at the ready. He emerges later with grubby hands and knees and a pocket full of bits of rock. I say rock, but of course there's more to it than that. I am, as always, amazed at the depth of his knowledge.

**19 November**
We work harmoniously side by side today, me trying to earn a living while Clive sorts out the photos from yesterday's adventure, handles some eBay admin and does a little gentle pottering. Then we have an early tea before a trip to the theatre – I know: another one! – this time to Northampton to see *Rain Man* starring Mathew Horne (of *Gavin & Stacey* fame) as Raymond, opposite Ed Speleers (formerly a footman in *Downton Abbey*) as Charlie, roles played in the film version by Dustin Hoffman and Tom Cruise respectively. It was mesmerising. Not bad for a Monday.

**20 November**
A brewing day. SMaSH brew bottled, Christmas ale started, redcurrant wine on the go. The kitchen floor is very, very sticky.

Clive takes a break to go out and give U3A another go. He comes back a couple of hours later knowing more than anyone needs to about the history of Christmas cards, 1840–1940.

## 21 November

The days are beginning to be less and less distinguishable for Clive. This is why I'm encouraging him to join something, so that there is a structure to his week. I know this is making me sound very controlling, but then I *am* very controlling. I just can't help myself. However, I really think it's important that he has a reason to get up in the mornings, so we have something to talk about at the end of the day.

On the plus side, though, he is keeping busy. The house has never been tidier and we are certainly eating well. For some unfathomable reason, Clive actually enjoys shopping for food, and I'm more than happy to let him do it.

## 22 November

I still haven't taken my new phone out of the house, because I don't want to scratch it or drop it. There's a reason they call me Little Miss Clumsy. I've lost count of the number of plates I've smashed on the mixer tap. I have, however, had a play with it and worked out what most of the little icons mean. Clive bamboozles me with talk of what I thought was sinking (which I'm definitely doing), but which turned out to be syncing (which I'm definitely not doing). My approach is to wait until I have a task, then find a way to solve it; Clive thinks I should become familiar with every function, just in case. One thing I know: I do not want to purchase anything from the Play Store. This, apparently, makes me odd.

## 23 November

An idle trawl for new beer recipes reveals one for Scottish Breakfast Stout, which contains chocolate, coffee and oats. I'll pass, thanks.

## 24 November

We have a his-and-hers morning. I go off to a yoga workshop and Clive goes to an USDAW meeting. One of us has a lovely time and comes home relaxed; the other comes home feeling the time has been wasted. We have a lazy afternoon, then pop along to the Arts Centre for Rolling in the Aisles. The first comedian is awful, the second one OK and the third one brilliant. Definitely worth a tenner.

## 25 November

All around the county the towns and villages are switching on their Christmas lights. (Did you just check the date of this entry? Yes, 25 November. Some people have no restraint.) With the Raunds Ukulele Orchestra I take part in that town's event, bashing out a few carols. There is a bit of a tricky moment when half of us go for the traditional arrangement of 'Santa Claus is Coming to Town' while the other half (the correct half) go for the full-on Springsteen, but I think we got away with it.

Clive has been tempted to come with me with the promise of mulled wine. Walking around all the stalls, it surprises me that there is a sort of petting zoo in one corner of the market square that includes a turkey.

'Come and see the lovely turkey, boys and girls. Doesn't he look tasty?'

This seasonal joy leads to conversation. Until this year there has always been a certain amount of ceremony surrounding Clive's last day at work before the festive break. He would come home and say, 'Christmas starts here!' and then we'd break out the Baileys and Quality Street, switch something mindless on the telly and settle in. This year there will be no such cut-off point. Will it be all right? I mean, we've already established that too much time together isn't good. My clients will close for business on 21 December and won't be back until 2 January. That's a long time to be sitting staring at each other. Clive suggests we find a huge and difficult jigsaw to keep us entertained. Has it come to this?

## 26 November

The annual pre-Christmas exploration of the deepest recesses of the freezer has revealed a lot of beetroot that I don't remember putting in there. There's also yet more soft fruit, so making blackcurrant wine is the chief task of the day. Is it starting to sound as though all Clive does is brew alcoholic drinks?

Joe pops in for a lunchtime sandwich and casually mentions that he and Caitlin will be having Christmas lunch with her family this year. That's OK, of course, but it will be the first time he won't be here. It's fine, really. No, really.

## 27 November

Today is all about parkin. Clive has found that the perfect recipe has made not one but two enormous slabs of the stuff. The idea is that it improves in the tin for about a week; this is not happening. We cut a small piece 'just to see if it's all right', then we cut another. This is why I married him.

The evening's yoga class proves to be a challenge. The hotel is hosting a conference and, despite assurances that the room the delegates are in has soundproofing, we struggle in the adjacent one. It sounds as though they might be playing hockey; the cheers and whoops certainly suggest some sort of competitive endeavour. We put on our best yogi smiles and try to focus. When we come to the end, I gather my students as close together as decency allows and get them to lie with their heads together, so they look like a flower. As our relaxation begins, the sound of 'Good Vibrations' permeates the dividing wall. Bless 'em, they don't even flinch.

## 28 November

The atrocious weather threatens to bring about the end of the world, so there is no possibility of taking a walk, as Charlotte Bronte would have said had she been in Kettering today. Clive looks gloomily through the window and decides it's not worth leaving the house. All he has on his agenda for the day is to stir the blackcurrant wine, which will take about 30 seconds. I panic. In the event he manages to find lots to do, just pottering about doing a bit of this and a bit of that, which of course as a retired gent he is entitled to do.

Inspired by the fact that his favourite jeans are a little snug, he takes a half-hearted look at the offerings of the various local gyms. Looking at the screen, he says: 'Where is the gym for old fat blokes like me?' It's true. All the pictures are of muscle-bound hunks and skinny women, none over 30.

It's not exactly encouraging. I have the same feeling when I look at some ads for yoga classes, where the illustration features someone who has apparently had her internal organs removed in order to perform the perfect Scorpion pose. Far better, surely, to have a picture of a 'normal' person, so we think, 'Well, if he/she can do it with a wobbly tum and baggy joggers, then so can I.'

He switches off without joining up.

## 29 November

The weather shows no signs of improving as mild wet stuff blows in from across the Atlantic. Today, however, Clive rolls up his sleeves and blitzes the kitchen with such gusto that I start to wonder if perhaps he's put the house on the market without telling me and we are to expect a viewing.

Meanwhile, there is a storm brewing online about a local pub that has renamed its upstairs function room as The Buddha Bar. Some of my Buddhist friends are understandably upset. As they point out, can you imagine a Jesus Joint, Mohammed's Nitespot or the Krishna Café? Or how about the Pope's Pizzeria? Actually, this last one doesn't sound that bad.

The evening brings ukulele rehearsal practice for me, but I come home despondent. Luckily, Clive is on hand with tea, sympathy and Maltesers. What do people do if they live on their own?

## 30 November

So we arrive at the six-month mark. I ask Clive how he thinks it's gone. Mostly fine, apparently. He likes being at home and spending more time with me (aw, shucks!), but is still missing the structure that working life provided. This is, of course, what I feared, but the solution is in his own hands. It would be easy – oh, so easy – for me to keep suggesting things for him to join, but I'm trying hard not to.

We seem to be managing OK for money thus far, but the stock market continues to bob up and down. I've given up watching the news, but I'm aware that parliament is to vote on the Brexit deal in a couple of weeks' time. What on earth is going on?

# DECEMBER

## 1 December

We set off in different directions this morning. I have my ukulele under my arm, on my way to play at (another) Christmas fair, this time at Vintage Retreat in Northampton. This is a massive building full of what some might call second-hand clothes and tat, but others would call treasures from days gone by. In the events hall in which we find ourselves there is a wondrous array of craft stalls. Mind you, while I might be impressed by the talent of the creatives behind them, there are only so many crocheted doilies and knitted Santa hats anyone needs.

Anyway, we set up and play our little hearts out, much to the bewilderment of the young women immediately opposite the stage who are selling hand-made organic cosmetics. They both film the whole thing on their phones. I can only imagine the text they add for their social media posts.

Meanwhile, Clive goes to the AGM of the county branch of the Labour Party. Somewhat to his surprise there are more people than seats, though 35-ish out of a potential 5,000 doesn't sound that impressive to me. It is, apparently, an interesting meeting, made surprisingly exciting by the unexpected announcement by the chairman that he doesn't want to stand for re-election. It is nice to have a glimpse behind the scenes of grassroots politics to compare and contrast with the chaos of the national picture.

With nothing that has to be done for the rest of the day, we settle down and watch a film, *Mr Holmes*, starring Ian McKellen, which proves to be an unexpected treat.

## 2 December

It's finally time for the first batch of mince-pies and, oh my, they're good. I have decided to ration myself to one a day. Today's is a reward for cleaning the house from top to bottom. These pastry delights are something of a speciality of Clive's. He makes his own mincemeat from scratch usually in September, or whenever the apples in our garden are ready for harvest. He adds various ingredients (I won't give away any secrets here, but there's always rum in there) and then leaves it to mature in a dark place until it's time to start preparing for the festive season. The pastry itself is very special, too, made with butter and just a touch of sugar. He makes enough in one batch to turn into 60 mince pies.

We go for a stroll around the park at dusk. So many people have their Christmas lights up already, which I think is much too early. Clive disagrees. Actually, we disagree about outside festive decoration in general. I tell him that he can do what he likes when he has his own house. One of our neighbours has an illuminated snowman wearing a Santa hat, which seems to cover all the bases.

### 3 December

With a view to buying a few Christmas presents, we pop over to Rushden Lakes, which is a shopping complex that has been built on what used to be a ski club. (No, that's not a misprint: a ski club in flat Northamptonshire.) The whole site stood empty and desolate for many years, but I have to say we weren't impressed by what has appeared. It is basically a massive clothes shop, with all the usual suspects: New Look, Next, H&M, White Stuff, River Island – you get the picture. But there is no bookshop, no music shop, no toy shop, no confectioner… I shall stick to the high street, thank you.

This afternoon Joe pops in to borrow the drill. I try not to laugh too much as he and Clive spend far longer than two intelligent men should trying to work out how to find the centre of a circle, so that the required hole is made in the right place.

## 4 December

It's cold but bright, so perfect digging weather. Clive sets off to the allotment with a bobble-hat in one hand and a flask of coffee in the other. He says he won't be long, but when I set off to teach four hours later there's no sign of him. It does cross my mind that he has perhaps fallen into a hole, but I don't have time to check. When I get home he has returned, but has clearly overdone things, feeling a little tender in the back and definitely achy.

There's no evening yoga tonight; after the fiasco of last week the class has been cancelled because the hotel is booked out to various parties. I toy with the idea of writing my Christmas cards, but in the end we find an old *Poirot* we haven't watched and doze fitfully through that instead.

## 5 December

It barely gets light, so there's nothing for it but to bottle up some more ale, then watch a film called *The Call of Cthulhu,* which is based on an H. P. Lovecraft story. It should come as no surprise, then, that it is strange.

That was Clive's day. I do lots of work but also treat myself to lunch out with Will. The café we go to is attached to a pick-your-own veg place and has a well-stocked shop selling seasonal fruit and veg grown on the farm. At this time of year, though, the shelves are mostly filled with extravagant pickles and hand-knitted reindeers. At the table next to us three women produce crackers from somewhere and wear their paper hats for the duration of their meal, not caring a jot that no one in the place is similarly attired. That's what you call style.

## 6 December
Bit of a dull day, really. The weather is neither t'other nor which, we have no post and the only people who ring are from 'Virgin' wanting to fix my internet connection by taking over my computer. I don't think so, thank you. The mood is lifted by Clive baking off another batch of mince-pies.

## 7 December
My mother rings, and we have a long conversation that includes the phrase 'fasting spittle'.

## 8 December
The Bookcave Limited was an independent bookshop in Kettering, but has moved to Wellingborough. Today, it is holding a grand relaunch and I've been invited to read a few pieces from my books, which they stock, alongside two performance poets. Chuck the Poet has

as usual pushed out the sartorial boat and is sporting a luxurious purple velvet jacket; Kezzabelle is resplendent in short skirt and fairy wings. I feel extremely dowdy. Do you know Amy Farrah Fowler in *The Big Bang Theory*? Yes, that.

I'm relieved that when my turn comes the audience laughs in all the right places. It's a pleasing-sized crowd, given it's a chilly Saturday morning. An added touch is that BBC Northampton turn up as part of *Treasure Quest*, a show in which presenters from the radio station take on a team from BBC Three Counties following clues that listeners have to solve. I've met presenter Jules several times now, and she obliges with a selfie. It never does any harm to have a little showbiz glitter sprinkled on proceedings.

## 9 December

I give in and let Clive bring the Christmas boxes down from the loft. This makes him very happy. While I stand my ground about it being too soon to put up the tree, I am prepared to let him decorate the front room window with some twinkling lights. So, while I settle down to write some cards, he busies himself sorting out tangled wires, checking timers and looking for extension leads. I have to concede that the results do look pretty.

Feeling festive, we break out the rum and settle down to watch *Nativity*, a gentle comedy made in 1992 and starring a very young-looking Martin Freeman;

actually, I supposed he *was* very young. It's hokum, but very nicely done.

## 10 December

We look something up on Clive's tablet and when we come to close down the screen he invites me to 'kiss out of it'. He means to click the 'x' in the top corner, of course, an 'x' being the well-known symbol for a kiss. Does anyone else say this, I wonder?

## 11 December

Clive has to be persuaded to leave the house. He manages to amuse himself all day with a bit of pottering, but eventually I have to kick him out.

'A walk will do you good,' I say.

He grumbles a bit but goes anyway. When he returns he says I was right. Fancy that.

## 12 December

While I'm busy at my computer, Clive gets his baker head on, big time: a couple of dozen banana scones for the freezer and about 60 gingerbreads, some shaped like Christmas trees.

I drag myself away to go and play my uke in an old folks' home. Actually, I don't suppose it's PC to call it that today, but there's no denying that it was a residential establishment for people in their later years. What else would you call it? The audience is cheery, due in no small part to the most enormous bottle of sherry

I've ever seen. Out of the corner of my eye I see that one of the ladies has managed to end up with a full glass in each hand. She drains one without pausing for breath, then looks about her for somewhere to put her empty glass. It goes in the bin, which I think is an elegant solution to the problem, and now, of course, she looks as though she's only had one drink.

## 13 December

Tearing my hair out a bit today as, in the usual pre-Christmas rush, I say to Clive, 'I want to retire and muck about all day like you do.'

'That's not fair,' he counters. 'I don't muck about *all* day, and anyway, I'm really happy.'

My envy levels rise.

There is time in the evening, though, to put up the Christmas tree and despite feeling a bit humbuggy I have to concede it looks great. As always, the accompaniment to this ceremony is the video of *The Muppet Christmas Carol*. Despite the rather grainy picture, we eschew the DVD version because one of the songs – 'The Love Has Gone' – has been cut. This is surely the best version ever made of the Dickens story, and in the role of Scrooge it has Michael Caine giving one of his finest performances.

## 14 December

I pop to the hairdresser for a pre-Christmas trim, where I'm told their boiler is on the brink and therefore the temperature of the water is likely to plummet without warning. And so it does. Then, swathed in an unflattering black gown I try not to look at my reflection as Kelly works her magic. We chat about the forthcoming festivities, and she tells me that in the interests of being green and saving a bit of money she is going to wrap all her presents in brown paper and decorate them with bits of ribbon. This sounds creative and laudable. I say as much: 'Yes, you can get a huge roll for tuppence ha'penny.'

'I have no idea what that means,' she says.

## 15 December

While I catch up on some work, Clive goes off to Nottingham for a day of talks from the British Geological Survey and comes home full of fascinating stories of silica mining and oil wells in Norfolk. I'm not being sarcastic here; it sounds like it was a really fascinating day.

He gets back just in time to meet me at the Arts Centre for *A Christmas Carol, as told by Jacob Marley (deceased)*. It is excellent, but the church is so cold that we can see our breath. Quite fitting for Dickens, I suppose. After the performance there is a Q&A with the actor James Hyland, but most of the audience flee in search of warmth and cheer elsewhere. A few of us stay and it is worth it, as he tells us the background to the show, his inspiration and so forth, and the fact that it takes 90 minutes to get the make-up and costume on, including terrifying contact lenses that complete the sepulchral look.

Back at home, with a mug of coffee laced with rum, we catch up on the *Strictly Come Dancing* final. Congratulations to Stacey and her professional partner Kevin, who is more tearful than she is. Bless him.

## 16 December

It's a big day as we reach the reason for all those dancetheatre rehearsals. It's show time and I'm performing in the catchily titled 'Deep Roots Tall Trees Changing Corby Project sharing and celebration of Polish culture'. There is a huge Polish community round here and the project is a collaboration of local music and cultural groups, of which the DRTT dancetheatre is one. Overall it is a very successful evening, although there is quite a lot of talking in the first half, exacerbated by the need to translate everything from/to Polish. However, the singing is extraordinary (in a good way) and we dancers do ourselves proud. Clive patiently sits through the whole thing in yet another cold church. As a reward, I say we can watch the final of *The Apprentice* in which Sian Gabbidon wins Lord Sugar's investment into her swimwear business. I'd have gone with the other finalist, who had a plan to conquer the world with nut milk, but what do I know.

## 17 December

For some reason we are both awake at five this morning, so I sneak down and make us a cuppa, knowing that a lie-in won't be a problem.

At 8.15 we wake for second time, but to the sound of someone ringing the doorbell with excessive vigour. Clive throws himself out of bed and down the stairs with unaccustomed speed and succeeds in clattering into the small table at the foot of the stairs and sending the newly installed Christmas lamp flying. On the other side of the front door Joe collapses in gales of laughter at his father's clumsiness and inventive use of expletives. Turns out he is here to pick up some drum paraphernalia.

He is not our only visitor today. A musician that I met at the Bookcave reading calls by to pick up a copy of *Nine Lives* and *Stripped-back Yoga* for his wife (she was with him in the bookshop and he wants to give them as a present). He stays for a cuppa and we chat about the possibility of him writing some music as background to me reading something and then posting in on YouTube. Might be fun.

Then brother Tim brings my mum down from Staffordshire for the ritual exchanging of Christmas presents. Mum has a battle going with the British Heart Foundation shop over their refusal to exchange an unopened pack of Christmas cards (don't ask), but a couple of hours later I get an email from her saying the matter has been resolved to her satisfaction as she has received a grovelling apology from the BHF head office. You can see where I get it from.

As if that wasn't enough excitement, Sam comes round for tea. I think he looks too thin, but he seems happy enough and has plenty of energy. I guess it's true that mums never stop worrying about their babies, even when they're six feet tall.

## 18 December

After all the disruption of yesterday, it's good to be able to spend the whole day working. I have lots to do before I finish for Christmas, and it helps that Clive goes off to do secret shopping for most of the afternoon, then settles down to watch an old episode of *Hornblower*. The evening's yoga class – which I nearly cancelled – brings only three students, but we have a nice time anyway.

## 19 December

I try to work because it's press day for one of my client magazines, but Clive is baking again and the aroma is very distracting. 'The girls' are coming round this evening and they are more interested in his pastry than in anything I have to say. Before that, though, we pop along to the Manor House Museum in town to nibble and natter with the Friends of said establishment. There is much sage nodding of white heads and we feel rather out of it, a mood not improved by the quiz that has picture clues to the identity of 20 artists. We only manage to guess seven.

## 20 December

Last-minute presents are bought and wrapped and menus finalised. This evening we head off to the Arts Centre for the annual 'Comedians and Carols' event with friends Terri and Russell, he of allotment fame. I'm sad to report it's a little disappointing this year, with a mediocre bill and very disruptive children on the row in front of us. Eventually I have to lean forward and growl through gritted teeth: 'Sit still!' They do. I can be very scary when roused.

## 21 December

Clive battles through the crowds to pick up some more food, because the shops will be closed for 24 hours and you never know. I tidy up some loose work ends. I have one more project to finish before close of play, but I fear it's going to run into tomorrow.

## 22 December

It does. I work until nearly 6pm to finish and send it to the client with a huge sigh of relief. Half an hour later the phone rings, but I ignore it. Two minutes later my phone signifies the arrival of an email. It's the client: he's delighted. I open a bottle of wine.

## 23 December

Another annual ritual is the Christmas gathering at Will and Tricia's house, where we reconnect with people we've known in passing for 30 years. This year's do is particularly splendid, because there are people we haven't seen for a while and it's lovely to catch up. It's official: Christmas has started.

## 24 December

Sam, Joe and Caitlin join us for dinner. The rice is a disaster and goes straight in the bin, but otherwise the evening is a great success. We play games and drink and chat and I remind myself and them how lucky we are to have such a stable family.

## 25 December

With no small children to consider, we allow ourselves a slow start to the day. Sam comes round mid-morning to open presents and to stay for lunch, of course. I have a magnificent haul of smellies, books and candles. Sam is pleased with the spray-painting station we've given him and Clive is surprised and really happy with the Fabulous Furry Freak Brothers comics I give him. Simple pleasures. After too much lunch and a little nap, we play Catan, a board game that Sam has given his dad. Then we settle down with the Quality Street to watch *Paddington 2*. A lovely day, despite there only being three of us.

The only shadow is that I learn that a fine fellow called Tony Pillage has died. This is a man I met only briefly (we had the same publisher), but who had a profound effect on me and, indeed, everyone he met. It's sad that he's gone, but it was his time – he suffered more than any man should – and since he was convinced he was destined for Valhalla, well, perhaps he's OK.

**26 December**

We continue what has become the habit of taking a turn around the park each morning. Today there is a family test-flying their new drone. Clive is so absorbed he doesn't look where he's going and comes perilously close to walking into a lamppost, much to the amusement of the people behind us. He styles it out. We also meet a cheery man in pyjamas and trainers, clutching a Cadbury's Chocolate Log. He says good morning and we pass. I resist the urge to stop him and ask what's going on in his life that has led him to this.

**27 December**

Debs comes over for lunch and a catch-up and we go for a walk around our part of town. We go past the end of the road where Joe and Caitlin live and I point out their house to her. Later, we learn there's been another body discovered in the flats at the end of the street: murder, apparently. They really need to think about moving somewhere else.

## 28 December

More walking today, this time around some Forestry Commission land with friends. It's cold, but we are well wrapped up and we do about four miles before returning to the house for mince-pies and cups of tea. There is also non-alcoholic hot punch and despite the absence of wine or spirits it makes me feel very sleepy. Back at home I succumb to a little nap before venturing out again, this time to a gathering of Poetry Group friends. We spend the evening playing music and putting the world to rights. On offer are more mince-pies and some very powerful chilli-stuffed olives. My contribution to the shared feast is some of Clive's home-made cheese straws, which one woman declares the best thing she has eaten all Christmas. I realise too late that I've forgotten to mention they contain butter, but what a vegan doesn't know can't hurt her.

## 29 December

To Staffordshire today, to check in on friends and relatives.

First port of called is Jenny and Ian. They welcome us with tea and mince-pies and we spend a lovely hour there catching up. Then it's on to brother Neil's house. I've told my sister-in-law Melanie that just a sandwich will be fine for lunch. She wilfully ignores this and puts on a splendid spread, as usual. Their teenage son Matthew is there, too, of course. Clive looks on enviously as he shows off his new snooker cue and the most amazing Lego Technic Bugatti Chiron. Make no mistake: just because it's Lego doesn't mean it's a toy. Mum is there, too, regaling us with U3A stories and town gossip in general. It's all going on in this sleepy market town!

It's grand to see everyone, of course, but it's nice to come home. Clive never says, but I'm sure he must feel overwhelmed by these trips when he has to face my lot mobhanded.

## 30 December

There is an unfortunate tradition in our house of having a massive row on New Year's Eve. This year we decide to get it over with a day early. We set off for a longish walk in relative harmony, but then what I think is a helpful suggestion is interpreted as nagging or interfering, probably both. The upside of this is that our fury makes us walk really quickly and the app on my phone rewards me with a fanfare and a virtual trophy for surpassing my fitness targets.

## 31 December

There is no fallout from yesterday. I'm not a sulker and if Clive is in a mood I choose to ignore it. A gentle stroll around Sainsbury's furnishes us with the wherewithal for this evening's meal.

We don't go out carousing, but instead, like the middle-aged couple we are, we play cards and listen to music, then switch on Jools Holland's' Hootenanny to see in the New Year. We watch other people's fireworks through the window, then retire. When all's said and done, it's an arbitrary date.

# JANUARY

## 1 January

I'm not given to making New Year resolutions, but today I decide that after the recent altercation I shall stop making suggestions about how Clive spends his time. This is already proving difficult. I wonder if there's an organisation to help control freaks like me.

'Good evening. My name is Julia and I'm a bossy cow.'

The Christmas decorations come down today and Clive goes mardy, as he always does on this occasion. He's just a big kid at heart.

## 2 January

It's back to work for me. I set the alarm for 7am and start the day with an hour's yoga and a healthy breakfast. At half eight I take Clive a cuppa in bed, because I'm kind. He is sitting up reading. It's all right for some.

## 3 January

A high-achievement day is further enhanced when we sign up for the challenge to walk 1,000 miles in a year. Not in one go – that would be ridiculous – but it works out at about 3 miles a day, which is surely doable. Remind me I said that in February, when it's cold and miserable and I don't want to leave the house.

## 4 January

There is absolutely nothing to report today. I work flat out all day and Clive keeps himself to himself doing I know not what.

## 5 January

Clive begins the day in style by dropping a casserole lid on to the tiled floor in the kitchen. This is before we've even had breakfast. It shatters to the four corners of the room. I can't grumble, not with my record. When we got married, back in the days when happy couples such as us would ask for modest household gifts rather than financial contributions towards a honeymoon in the Bahamas (don't get me started), we received 13 casserole dishes. Needless to say, most of them are long gone. This last one is triangular and therefore only really used for keeping leftovers in, and even that has lost its lid along the way. Nevertheless, I shall miss it when I eventually drop it.

Second mishap comes after dinner. We don't usually eat on our knees in front of the TV, but today we do. Big mistake. Clearing the pots away, Clive sends the bowl of rice and peas flying. Again, I can't grumble. He is very cross with himself and, as I point out, it could have been worse: could have been the sweet 'n' sour sauce.

These things come in threes. Clive goes into the kitchen to make some tea and I hear a loud 'Oi-yer-bugger-man!' No, he hasn't dropped something else; this exclamation comes in response to the kettle going bang and emitting a huge blue flash.

## 6 January

First job of the day is to buy a replacement kettle. When Sunday trading was first introduced, I was dead against it. My standards have slipped and while I wouldn't go and do a supermarket shop, I will occasionally pop out for something that just can't wait, and I can't wait for a new kettle. I don't know why it is, but tea made with water boiled in a saucepan just isn't the same. We join the throngs in Argos, where a disgruntled couple are returning a Dyson. I hope it wasn't her Christmas present from him.

## 7 January

Until today I have been writing this diary in secret. I've told a couple of friends but warned them of dire consequences should they reveal it to anyone. The reason is not that I'm being sneaky, but that I didn't want Clive to start acting the part by doing deliberately daft things. I needn't have worried on that score. I was also a bit concerned that he might be offended. For some reason, today seems the day to tell him what I'm up to and as I go out of the door to an evening meeting I leave him with June to read through.

When I return he has read the pages and is pleased with what I've done. I shouldn't have doubted him. He is always very supportive of what I write. I wonder if I would be so generous were the roles reversed.

## 8 January

Clive continues to entertain me without having to try. From four rooms away (he is in the kitchen and I am at my desk at the back of the house), I hear him embark on one of his sneezing fits. My late father was no slouch in the sneezing department, once giving vent 19 times in a row without pausing. However, while Dad was a tidy, kittenish sneezer, Clive expires with such force it's a wonder a small crowd doesn't gather to see what all the noise is. It's not just the actual sneeze, but also the little groan after each one, a sort of steadying of the buffs before the next onslaught.

Once he's finished, he staggers into the office, exhausted. 'I'm not putting it on,' he says. 'Did you know that a sneezing fit is the closest you come to death without actually dying?'

I doubt this is true.

## 9 January

'Try this,' says Clive, thrusting a small wine glass of wine under my nose.

You know that face a baby pulls when you try to give it rhubarb? Yes, that was my response. Now, it could have been because I'd just cleaned my teeth, but this latest offering from the Thorley winery tasted like cheap cooking sherry. Clive is crestfallen, so I try to find something positive to say, but can't. On the other hand, the vegetable soup he serves up for lunch is amazing. Yin and yang.

The day's post brings an invitation to look round a new care home for the elderly and infirm. Fill in your own pithy remark here.

## 10 January

To my amazement, Clive announces his intention to join a Tai Chi class this evening. What is more amazing is that he actually does. He returns home having learned how to be an Eagle, a Bear, a Dragon and who knows what else. He has enjoyed himself. This could be the start of something good.

## 11 January

In a fanciful moment I remark that through the window I can see an amazing cloud formation that looks like an escarpment, with the sun just peeping up over the top. Clive, ever the scientist, says, 'Yes, that's an occluded front,' and proceeds to give me a mini lecture on weather. Is my life richer for this knowledge?

## 12 January

Another his-and-hers kind of day. I go off to a women's self-defence course, and Clive stays in to do various brewing tasks. When I come home I find he has also tidied his desk. Can it be that time of year again already?

In the evening we go to the theatre to the opening night of *Our Lady of Kobeho*, a worthy piece about three Rwandan schoolgirls who claim to have visions of the Virgin Mary. It's very good, but a touch on the long side and the theatre is very warm. I struggle to stay awake.

## 13 January

I'm reading *Thinking On My Feet* by Kate Humble and now I want to go and live in the Wye Valley with her. This isn't practical, so instead we go for a lovely walk on the edge of the county that runs up to Cambridgeshire. It's blustery, but mostly dry. We hardly see a soul.

For dinner, Clive tries out a new vegetarian main course, a sort of chickpea-based stew with really claggy dumplings on top. It is lovely, but leaves us feeling very full. We doze gently in front of the telly for the rest of the evening.

## 14 January

Clive continues to enjoy the reruns of *Hornblower*. This leads him to announce his intention to start doffing an imaginary cap in thanks or greetings, as appropriate, in the manner of a sea captain in a tricorn hat. This is either an affectation or a touch of old-world charm. You decide.

## 15 January

The weather continues to be unseasonably mild, despite dire warnings in the news about the approach of Beast from the East #2. Clive trots off to the allotment, leaving me in peace. He comes home three hours later, tired but happy, and clutching a few small but well-intentioned leeks. In celebration of this horticultural achievement, we finish the jigsaw that Mum gave us for Christmas.

## 16 January

Worn out by yesterday's exertions, Clive potters aimlessly today, which I don't let annoy me. Honestly. I find it difficult to settle to much work and resort to what I euphemistically call catching up on a bit of admin. The main thing I catch up on, however, is listening to Radcliffe & Maconie, whose BBC Six Music show has been shunted from weekday afternoons to weekend mornings. Now, I love this show, but I'm not prepared to get up at 7am on a Saturday to hear it. This is what the internet is for.

On this otherwise largely aimless day, Clive announces his intention to go to Shrovetide in February. To explain: he spent most of his childhood in Ashbourne in Derbyshire (where I was born, too) and every year on Shrove Tuesday and Ash Wednesday there is a massive football match between the up'ards and the down'ards, who live on opposite sides of the river. The goals are three miles apart. It's a lively event that involves much physical contact between participants and spectators alike, falling in the river and a lot of drinking. There are some arcane rules, but I have no idea what they are, despite my having been several times.

This year, Clive is going without me and is planning to meet up with old friends. I hope he has a splendid time, but I'm not a great fan of going back. I'd rather remember things as they were – or as I think they were – than to revisit them and be disappointed.

**17 January**
Clive's sole achievement today is to clean the shower, giving it what he calls a 'good scogging'. Ignoring the fact that this is casting aspersions on my own efforts in this department, he strips to the bare essentials and wades in, wielding a cocktail of cleaning liquids until he can see his face in the porcelain. This is all well and

good, but he then leaves the window wide open to let out the chemical fumes, so when I go up later to use the facilities it's like walking into a freezer. This annoys me far more than it has any need to.

He does, though, go to Tai Chi again, wearing a new t-shirt. Both these events are noteworthy.

## 18 January

Clive announces today that it is too cold to do anything and he has caught my 'hibernation gene'. My response to this is to drag him out for a walk round the park. Despite a steel-grey sky, it's not too bad out: very cold, but not cold enough to numb the chin. Our trip coincides with school chucking-out time and we despair at the sight of so many parents clutching their phones rather than their child's hand. However, rounding the corner we encounter a jovial man pushing a toddler in a buggy and discussing the merits or otherwise of trying to eat sandwiches in the bath. Order restored.

## 19 January

An impromptu walk around Market Harborough, through the park then back through the side streets, takes us past a shop selling nothing but lights. We've been searching for a lamp to stand in the corner of our living room and they have just the thing. It is more expensive than we had been hoping for, but we throw caution to the winds and order one.

Clive cooks with paneer for the first time and is pleased with the results. I must say I do like having a personal chef. Then it's out to comedy night at the Arts Centre, where one of the acts is called Olaf Falafel. No, really. His jokes are as funny as his name.

## 20 January

Clive goes out on his own again! This time is to the HQ of the British Geological Survey for a meeting and a tour of the core store. This is exactly like it sounds: a huge warehouse where the BGS stores all the core samples that have ever been taken in the UK. Clive is pleased beyond measure at this opportunity. On the down side, that cold that has been threatening on the sidelines has landed and he spends the evening coughing and spluttering while I'm trying to watch *Vera*. I despatch him to the spare room.

## 21 January

He definitely has a cold. I am sent out to buy Night Nurse, Day Nurse, cough medicine and tissues. The pharmacist is sympathetic.

'Your husband, you say? Ah, yes, I understand.' He gives me a twinkling smile. 'What he needs is plenty of attention, maybe unlimited access to Netflix and lots of cups of tea.'

He also sells me a variety of drugs, but concedes that the best thing Clive can do is just stay in until the cold goes away.

## 22 January

The cold persists, so Clive decides the best place for him is bed (and I'm inclined to agree). I leave him with his mobile by his side in case he needs to summon a Lemsip. I am not a good nurse, but I do my best, plumping up pillows and so forth while trying not to get too close.

## 23 January

Day three of the Worst Cold Ever and Clive manages to get dressed today, and even to cook himself a piece of toast while I'm out teaching. Worn out by the effort, he settles down in front of a film and manages to stay awake for the whole thing. I think we might be through the worst of it. However, three days of tossing and turning in a fever have done incredible things to his hair. What with that and the lack of strength to shave, he is starting to look like, well, I was going to say the Wild Man of Borneo, but a quick Google leads me to think this might be inappropriate. While searching, though, I come across this gem of information: *'Head-hunting stopped around 70 years ago on Borneo, but authorities are believed to have turned a blind eye to it during World War II, when the victims were often Japanese soldiers.'* There's a thing.

## 24 January

Clive continues to make slow but steady progress from the pit of despair. I encourage him to come round the park with me: 'The fresh air will do you good,' I say. It takes a while to get him sufficiently wrapped up to brave the elements, but he admits it is worth the effort.

It occurs to me today that it would have been better if, as the government had originally promised me, I was also counting down to retirement, but instead of nine months I have six years before I get my state pension. Nevertheless, I've started to look for ways I can cut down on my hours without losing too much money. This reflection has been prompted by various bad news stories relating to the health of people in my life. What if I work until I'm 66, then one or other of us keels over? What will it all have been for?

## 25 January

Going from strength to strength today, Clive ventures into town with me. The fridge contains nothing more than some white pastry fat, a lump of sad Cheddar and, inevitably, a wizened carrot in the 'beer tray' at the bottom. We venture to Sainsbury's and, while I dash off in search of hot chocolate and gravy browning, I entrust to Clive the task of choosing some fruit. I return a few minutes later to find him trapped at the banana station, fenced in by the trolley of a ferocious-looking woman who is glaring at him as though he has taken too long to choose between organic and merely Fairtrade. He looks bewildered; he's been out of circulation too long. I rescue him, and buy him a pound of chipolatas to make up for the trauma.

## 26 January

It's another of those his-and-hers days today, as I go to a meeting of Corby Collective Poets and Clive goes to a union meeting. I have the more rewarding time.

## 27 January

We gird our loins and venture into the chilly afternoon for an elongated lap of the park. Most of the way we walk in the sort of companionable silence that only a couple that have been together 40 years can enjoy. Then I feel compelled to say that I wish I could retire, too. Far from feeling annoyed that he is having fun while I'm working, I'm annoyed that I have to work while he is having fun. It's a subtle distinction, but what it means is that he's made the right decision and I'm cursing the government (again) for changing the rules. Truth be told, we could perhaps limp along on a diet of bread and cheese if I wasn't working, but that doesn't appeal. Overall, I'd rather work then play, rather than not work and not be able to afford to play. Fickle? Yes.

## 28 January

So today he feels giddy. Oh for goodness sake! I do check in with the pharmacist just in case, but he reassures me that it's all part of the particular cold that's doing the rounds.

'His tubes are full,' he says. 'Olbas oil and steam is the thing. That, and time.'

I toy with the idea of asking for a prescription for myself: *200mg caplets of Patience, to be taken as required.* I am a rubbish nurse and an intolerant wife.

## 29 January

Our new sofa arrives today, which we have bought from a local independent furniture store. One of the major chains told us proudly, 'All our stock is made in China.' Well, the one we've bought was made in Bedford. Two jolly fellows unload it into the front room for me and take off the plastic wrapping with a flourish. The sofa has a wobble. I am complimented on my use of the word 'kibble' and my ability to produce a hammer. Neither helps. There is much tugging of beards. The boss is summoned. More pondering and head scratching. The bally thing has to go back.

Later, watching *Winterwatch*, Clive observes, 'Chickens can't float.'

## 30 January

Yesterday it was the sofa, today it's the washing-machine. I don't have much luck with them. I don't know why. I don't abuse them by washing football boots in them or overstuffing them with quilts. Anyway, the current machine is less than a year old and has started to make what can only be described as a graunching noise. I've heard this noise before and I know it's the bearings going.

Clive makes a quick call to the retailer, pointing out that this machine is still under guarantee and a man arrives to take a look at the job. The man – let's call him Ted – listens patiently while Clive describes the symptoms, and then gives the drum a spin.

He says, 'No, it can't be the bearings.' He pulls the machine out from under the worktop, pokes about in its innards and says again, 'No, it's not the bearings.'

Clive fetches two bath towels, wets them in the sink and puts them on to spin. The graunching begins.

Ted is triumphant. 'Ah yes, it's the bearings. I thought so.'

What a good job he was on hand to diagnose the problem.

## 31 January

The cold continues, not only the weather, but also the germs infecting Clive. Enough already, on both counts.

Some parts of the country are undoubtedly suffering from the effects of the weather, but as so often seems to be the case it's largely left our county alone. The way the media are banging on, though, you'd think there were drifts up to the windowsills. This particular piece of hyperbole is a family joke, as it was something Flora (Clive's late mum, remember?) was fond of saying.

She had a lot of these gems in her vocabulary – for instance, whenever we're out in the car in the rain we always say, 'I think we'll drive through it,' which reminds us of an ill-fated trip around Ladybower

Reservoir where the heavens opened, but Flora, bless her, was determined to have a good time. Hence the somewhat misplaced optimism.

She would also describe anyone who irritated her as 'a bugger up the back', presumably without any sense of what this actually means.

# FEBRUARY

## 1 February

Today we are very sad to learn that comedian Jeremy Hardy has died from brain cancer. He was only 57. I don't usually pay much heed to celebrity news, but this upsets me more than the death of a stranger should. He was a stalwart of many of my favourite Radio 4 shows and I've seen him live three times. He was wonderful and will be much missed.

**2 February**

It is apparently World Ukulele Day. Where do these things come from? Is there a UN committee somewhere that sits twice a year and decides that, yes, National Sandwich Awareness Week is worthy, but International Fence Post Day might be a step too far?

I go to an author gathering with my publisher, which inspires me to come home and crack on with my writing. In the evening we go to hear comedian Robert Newman at the Arts Centre, whom you might remember as one half of Newman and Baddiel. This man is a genius. His use of language makes me think there's no point in my ever writing anything again.

**3 February**

A reluctant Clive accompanies me on a walk around Prologis Park, the rather grandly named industrial estate on the edge of town. I know what you're thinking: that perhaps I've spent too long editing articles for logistics publications and have finally had my head turned by a nicely appointed warehouse. However, while the warehouses are undoubtedly there, they are set in a thoughtfully landscaped environment that means if you don't lift your head too high you can't see them over the trees. There are footpaths and waterways, picnic tables and nesting boxes and it's much nicer than it sounds. We clock up a gentle four and a half miles, then undo all the good work by popping into the Co-op, where we buy a cut-price lemon drizzle cake teetering on the verge of its best-before date.

After a particularly spicy barbecue pork dish, Clive has a monumental sneezing fit that uses up more calories than our walk. I wonder if I should get him looked at?

Unable to resist, I've just Googled this and find it is a real thing called 'gustatory rhinitis'. Amongst the advice is the suggestion that eating smaller meals might help. Shall I tell him?

## 4 February
The battle over the washing-machine grows. Having persuaded Currys PC World that we need a replacement machine, Clive visits the store to set the wheels in motion. However, those wheels, not unlike the machine itself, grind exceeding slow and, despite having the requisite code for the transaction, there is a delay for some unspecified technical reasons. Now Clive's teeth are also grinding.

## 5 February
Clive decides he's not strong enough to ring up about the washing-machine and instead spends the day pottering and mostly doing a jigsaw. It is fortunate that I have a full day's teaching ahead of me and therefore don't have the opportunity to nag him about such indolence. On the other hand, when I do eventually get

home and collapse in a heap, there is pizza waiting for me, so I suppose I shouldn't grumble.

## 6 February
The home brewery is in full swing today, which means visiting the kitchen is pretty much by appointment only. Every surface seems to be covered with old towels, buckets and bits of tubing, and a mighty bottling task is in full swing. I am not allowed to move anything, not even to reach for a mug. I retreat to safety at the back of the house.

## 7 February
Today there is a lot of sighing. After the activity of yesterday, Clive does nothing today, while I hurtle around in my usual way. My anxiety levels are higher than usual because in my capacity as judge I'm speaking and presenting prizes at the H E Bates Short Story Competition Awards Evening later, and I'm apprehensive. I don't know why; it's a low-key affair and the audience is unlikely to be hostile. Nevertheless, I try on all my clothes before settling on an outfit that I hope gives the impression that I'm intelligent and professional, but also a bit funky. The photos of the event reveal that I look like my mother.

Meanwhile, Clive and Sam go to the Arts Centre for a comedy night, a fundraiser for a project in Moldova. On the bill are James Acaster, Josh Widdicombe, Ed

Gamble and Milton Jones. They definitely have more fun than me.

**8 February**
The replacement washing-machine will be delivered next Monday, sometime between 8am and 6pm. I shall not hold my breath. Also expected today is the delivery of the replacement sofa, which I'm more confident about.

Clive surprises me by declaring that he has a favourite saucepan.

The big news, though, is that Storm Erik is coming! Heavy rain and wind are forecast, and the BBC weather bods helpfully point out: 'There will be frost and the chance of some snow in the north of the country towards the end of the weekend when falling rain meets cold air.' Anyone would think it was winter.

Curious about why storms have names anyway, I discover that the Met Office decided to start giving storms boys' and girls' names back in 2014, in the same way that they do in America. The first windstorm to be named was Abigail on 10 November 2015. The theory is, according to the BBC website, that naming big storms will make people more aware of them and how dangerous they can be, and make it easier to follow the progress of a storm on TV, the radio or social media. Good lord.

## 9 February

I don't know what Clive gets up to during the day, because I'm out and about, first at a poetry group meeting, then just doing chores. In the evening, though, he gets himself in my good books by accompanying me to a gathering (I can't say party, really) of arty friends where there is plenty of conversation, but not much alcohol to smooth the way. Nevertheless, Clive throws himself into things and is surprised by how much he enjoys himself. There is a bring-and-share buffet, an option that always has the potential to go either way, but tonight's is very tasty. There is some explosive Sri Lankan dhal, which, curiously, does *not* make Clive sneeze.

## 10 February

Today is a completely blank day. Nothing happens at all, never mind anything amusing. I suppose you could say it's an opportunity to sit and relax, to regroup and focus on the important things in life. Or you could say it's a really boring day.

## 11 February

The new sofa has been delivered on time, as promised, with a smile and another apology. That's what you call service.

The evening is enlivened by a trip to the theatre to see *Caroline's Kitchen*, a comedy by Torben Betts starring Caroline Langrishe and Aden Gillett. You might not know their names, but you'd know their faces from, as the programme helpfully points out, *Lovejoy*, *Judge John Deed* (her) and *The House of Eliott* (him). This rather suggests that neither of them has done anything for the last 20 years, which is clearly not the case. I wonder how it feels to be identified by your appearance in one particular TV series.

We are pleased to note that, as usual, many of the supporting cast have appeared in *Casualty* and/or *Holby City*. No disrespect is intended by this observation, by the way; it's just that we always check who has endured what must surely be a rite of passage to play 'grieving relative in waiting room' or 'burns victim #1'.

## 12 February

Standing at the sink and gazing through the kitchen window, I despair at the sight of the woman from the house over the road out in the street in her dressing-gown and slippers pouring boiling water from her kettle on to the frozen windscreen of her car. There goes the neighbourhood.

## 13 February

There's brewing in earnest today, which means the house smells amazing. I am rather concerned that I might be taking the smell of hops and malt around with me, but if any of my yoga students notice they are too polite to say, or possibly embarrassed on my behalf.

Clive dismisses a cold-caller: 'Take me off your database, there's a good boy.' It is to the caller's credit that he laughs.

**14 February**
Today's challenge comes courtesy of Clive's tablet. It is a touchscreen device, but today it steadfastly refuses to respond, no matter which finger is used or how much pressure is applied. Tempers fray. After many exploratory phone calls to legitimate help sources, including the manufacturer, the retailer and even Google (it being an Android device), Clive eventually goes into town and takes it to a dodgy-looking phone shop run by Jimmy the Fish, or some such character, who diagnoses pixel problems and says a new screen should fix it. His quote is reasonable ('Cash only, squire), so somewhat against his better judgement Clive leaves the device there, to be collected next week.

By agreement we don't bother with any Valentine's Day shenanigans. The occasion should, we feel, be left to those in the first flush of romance, not crusties like us who have known each other for 40 years.

**15 February**
The staff in Vision Express find out that I'm not a woman to be trifled with. They mess me about and make me so angry that I have to retire to Bewiched for a mug of tea and a slice of millionaire's shortbread until I calm down. Suffice to say I don't have my intended

appointment and by the time I have walked home I have decided to cancel my direct debit payment for my contact lenses and take my business elsewhere. I am too long in the tooth to endure poor customer service when there are so many other opticians to choose from. Not that they'll care, of course, but it makes me feel better.

Sensing that the safest option would be to leave me in on my own for a while, Clive goes off to do a supermarket run and comes back with a bottle of white wine, a tub of Pringles and a Cadbury Creme Egg. How well he knows me.

## 16 February

I decide a walk is in order. Clive has some fancy Ordnance Survey app that is supposed to make route-planning easier, but today it isn't working and he spends a long time fannying about with it rather than getting out a paper map, which to my mind would have been the obvious solution. I get cross; he gets defensive. We eventually set off, but by then I'm in a proper grump.

However, Mother Nature works her magic and it's not long before I start to feel better and by the time we have eight miles under our boots I am positively cheerful. We end up walking along the edge of the Boughton House estate, which is the domain of the Duke of Buccleuch. It's very beautiful, and there are lots of people about enjoying the early spring sunshine, a scene only marred by the discovery of a swan corpse. Nature red in tooth and claw, as they say.

## 17 February

Today is Sam's birthday. How can we be old enough to have a thirty-year-old son? He comes over for lunch and to open his cards and presents, which still come to our house despite him having been in his own home for several years. Clive excels in the cake-making department, but is rather annoyed that I let Sam take away what we don't eat.

## 18 February

Well, the washing-machine arrives, but the delivery driver steadfastly refuses to take away the packaging, despite this being part of his job. I know it is; I check. I ring the company customer service line for a stern word, at the end of which conversation I have secured a £30 voucher in compensation for my trouble and the promise that the packaging will be picked up, but not until Monday. Is it worth it, I wonder? Why do I get so agitated about things that don't matter a jot in the grand scheme? It's not just me this time, though. Clive is equally discouraged by the state of events.

'Sometimes,' he says, 'I think there's only you and me who care about anything. The world is full of wankers.'

Better news on the tablet front, however. Despite my fears that the phone shop was probably a front for some nefarious gangland activity, the device is returned in full working order. We'll gloss over the angst of reloading all the apps.

The evening brings more celebrations as Sam, Joe and Caitlin join us for a curry, where Clive takes advantage of eating out to order not only a crab starter, but also a prawn main course. I try not to look. I order vegetable biryani and am quick to point out that it so much better than the one Clive attempted back in September. Not that I harp on about things.

## 19 February

In a case of role reversal, I can't settle today. I have lots of work to do, which I manage, but I find it hard to find any joy in my job. Clive, meanwhile, gets through all sorts of tasks inside and outside the house. We have a huge Hebe just outside the back door. At least we did have. Clive has set about it with the loppers and now there is just a stump where once there was luxurious foliage. Apparently this is going to do it good.

What makes this burst of energy all the more remarkable is that Clive was up until half two, not, as you might be thinking, because of a seafood-induced malady, but because he was on the Royal Mint website in a queue to buy a silver £2 coin featuring a coloured image of the Gruffalo. These coins are part of a highly collectable set and often sell on for way over their original price. He logs on to the site just before midnight to discover that he is already 13,000th in the queue. He's committed, though, so sits there until finally it's his turn. I just hope it's worth it.

**20 February**

It pleases me no end this morning to see a young lad of about ten riding a unicycle around the park.

There is more mirth to be hand in H&M, where a large woman is bending down to read the bottom hanger on the underwear rail and when she rises her rear sends an entire display of satin camisoles careering across the shop. It's not nice to laugh at another's misfortune, but come on!

Clive devotes his energy to doing something with the residual stock of butternut squash that has been overwintered in the spare room since September and is now on the verge of going soft. Several kilos of pulp are now residing in the freezer and as I type this there is a batch of cheesy squash scones rising nicely in the oven. I shouldn't really have one – I've just had yet another Creme Egg and fear that I might be developing a bit of a fondant habit – but it would be rude not to when he's gone to so much trouble.

**21 February**

Clive steps in to deliver a set of proofs to a client for me, which he's happy to do because the office is close to his old workplace. He pops in to say hello to 'the lads', who all greet him the same way: 'My, you're looking well,' which he interprets as 'Blimey, you've put on some weight.' This notwithstanding, he comes home very relieved that he doesn't have to stay for the rest of the shift.

## 22 February

Having seen his former colleagues yesterday, Clive is shocked to receive a phone call telling him that one of them has lost his wife suddenly this morning. Just 61 and with no obvious signs of illness, she had a heart attack and died on the spot. This is very sad, not least because the man in question had been putting off retiring so that his pension pot was as big as possible to give him and his lady the best possible time in their dotage. Makes you think.

## 23 February

More bad news today, as we learn that our allotment neighbour Malcolm has died. Galvanised to make the best of the time we have, we set off for a walk across the fields. I'm very fond of Northamptonshire, but it's not blessed with the most inspiring of views. It's very pretty in a rolling-English-countryside sort of way, but sometimes I miss the Staffordshire hills. Nevertheless, there is a lovely spring feel to the air and the birds and bees are out and about. We stop to try to take some photos of the red kites, but they move too fast and we end up with a couple of dozen pictures of squares of blue sky.

For our evening's entertainment, foregoing the grand final of *The Greatest Dancer*, which is the best the BBC can offer for prime-time Saturday viewing (someone called Ellie won, if you're interested), we go to the Royal for the preview night of *The Remains of the Day*. Neither of us has read the book or seen the film, so we are able to watch and enjoy the play on its own merits.

There is a bit of sport before the curtain rises. We are directed to our seats, E12 and E13, but find someone has left a jacket and some papers in one of them. Clearly they belong to a reviewer or possibly a member of the production team, so Clive picks them up and nurses them in anticipation of their owner returning to claim them in due course.

Sure enough, a flustered chap comes rushing in and says, with no preliminaries, 'You're in my seat and that's my stuff!'

Clive points out that we are in the correct seat, but the fellow is not appeased. He gets out his ticket: 'Look! E12. You're wrong.'

He does indeed have the right seat number, but unfortunately for him his ticket is for the circle and we are in the stalls. He harrumphs, grabs his belongs and storms off, without so much as an apology or even a sheepish grin. Well, really!

### 24 February

We are enjoying a lovely mild spell; the weatherman says it's more like May than February and I'm inclined to believe him, since even I went for my morning constitutional without a coat. Clive and Paul go for a round of golf and I potter at home, with the garden doors wide open. I even take my coffee out on to the garden bench. Clearly the neighbours think spring has sprung, because more than one has dusted off the mower. There is a *RUM-rum-RUM-rum* coming from someone's petrol machine that desperately needs something adjusted to make it run more smoothly and less annoyingly.

A quick trawl on Facebook reveals that someone I know has set up a crowdfunding page for her son's birthday. How did we come to this?

To take our minds off the parlous state of the world, we go to a comedy night with our friend Debs. It's part of the Leicester Comedy Festival but is being held in Market Harborough: to be precise, in the market hall. Yes, that's the building where they have the market. The comedians seemed to find it hilarious that they have to walk through the butcher's shop to get to the stage, but that's showbusiness! It was a really good night and just what was needed.

## 25 February

The world is celebrating today, because Olivia Colman has won the Best Actress Oscar for her role in *The Favourite*. There was no host for the ceremony this year, but it didn't seem to matter. If anything, it rather improved proceedings.

Closer to home, the mild weather continues and the birds are well and truly twitterpated, as Thumper would have it. I watch in awe as a lone blackbird overcomes a flock of starlings who have designs on the spoils on the bird table. Once the coast is clear, a couple of tomtits come and view the nesting box outside my window, but after popping in and out a few times they shake their heads in disappointment and fly away. Clearly, my garden is not the des-res I think it is.

## 26 February

I have two friends who are having treatment in hospital today. One posts a picture on Facebook of her NHS ward. Oh dear. The other friend is also having NHS treatment, but in the private hospital down the road. I don't know how this works: some kind of lucky dip, perhaps. He is given a private room with TV and tea and lovely sandwiches after what we shall call here a small procedure.

## 27 February

The mild weather continues, which is either a lovely treat or the beginning of the end, depending on which newspaper you read. Honestly, some days you wonder why you've got out of bed, because there's so much doom and gloom everywhere. When it's not Brexit, it's the climate emergency or the resurgence of measles. Nevertheless, I paint on a smile and look forward to dancetheatre in the evening. It should have been a taster session for new members, but in the event only one new person ventures in. We're not surprised. Two of my friends had said they would come along, but neither does or offers any reason for her absence, which is disappointing. Why are people so flaky?

Clive goes off to a meeting of the local archaeology society and returns having won the raffle again: this time two bottles of beer, which is the last thing he needs, but as he points out it is better than a tin of fruit salad in syrup.

## 28 February

Malcolm's funeral today was well attended. When you only know someone from one point of view, it's always interesting to hear what else they'd had in their life. It amuses Clive no end to learn that Malc had two Mercedes vehicles: a 4x4 monster for use at the allotment and a snazzy saloon for going to Waitrose. He'll be missed.

Sam comes round and is feeling a bit glum, so we sit and watch *The Muppets*, the film from 2011, which definitely does the trick.

## MARCH

### 1 March

Some women want diamonds; all I want is three new fence panels for the back garden. These are delivered and we set to and install them. As we finish, our neighbour comes out to congratulate us on a job well done, and at such speed! I'm just amazed we managed it without any swearing. Clive treats himself to part one of the *Lord of the Rings* trilogy. I will do anything to avoid watching this. I just don't get it, sorry.

## 2 March
We blitz the house in a frenzy of cleaning. I set off, then Clive follows me round with the hoover. As a reward, he gets to watch *Lord of the Rings* part two.

The evening brings comedy again, this time Patrick Monahan at the Arts Centre. The audience is small but appreciative. One of my yoga students sits behind me and just for a moment I wonder if perhaps I should be sipping mineral water rather than downing a pint of Pot Belly Brewery's Pigs Do Fly, but I'm halfway through it so it's too late to worry about my reputation. At the end of the evening, Clive produces a carrier bag from his pocket and proceeds to gather up not just our empties but also other people's. The staff here know about his brewing hobby, so they line up the bottles on the bar and he sweeps up as many as he can carry. This means that he clanks ominously as we walk home. I hope my student isn't watching.

## 3 March
OK, universe, enough! Another of our circle has died in his sixties. In the spirit of not wasting a moment, Clive watches *Lord of the Rings* part three, while outside Storm Freya threatens to blow us all to oblivion. As the night draws in, a crash has us rushing to the back door to see what the damage is. The new bird table is on its side and

the pop-up greenhouse has broken free from its moorings. It is only the presence of a strategically placed brick that has prevented it from setting off down the road on its own. It is banging against the back gate as though it expects it to fall open, but instead we retrieve it and pin it back in place with a couple of dustbins. Crisis averted.

## 4 March

My editorial reverie is interrupted by Clive bringing me a small glass of something red.

'Try this,' he says. 'Tell me what you think.'

What he means, of course, is 'Tell me how good this is.' I take a sip and try not to wince as the sample of fruity wine attacks every nerve ending in my mouth.

'Mm, not bad. Perhaps a little on the dry side?'

He is indignant: 'It's supposed to be dry. I like it dry.'

I backtrack: 'It will be lovely with a dash of soda water in, or perhaps some lemonade.' It's hard to tell if this suggestion makes things better or worse.

## 5 March

Breakfast is punctuated by the sound of corks popping off the wine that was bottled yesterday. I make no comment.

Clive is excited today because he's off on his much-anticipated trip to Ashbourne for the annual Shrovetide Football event. He will see old friends and rekindle his youth. I shall miss him, of course, but these occasions of separation are important and valuable. You can have too much of a good thing. And talking of trips…

On my way back from the Co-op, I see my neighbour's dog hurtling down the street towards me, followed by the neighbour herself, shouting at the dog to come back. I do what any decent person would do and lunge at the dog as he attempts to jink past me. I manage to get a very loose hold on his collar, but this doesn't slow his momentum and he threatens to escape my grasp by pulling into the road. I pull back and in the process clatter to the ground. What began as a heroic dive ends as an undignified sprawl. Of course, the sensible thing would have been to put down my shopping and use both hands to grab him in the first place, but I didn't do that. OK, I saved the dog, but I ripped the knee of my jeans and my actual knee and scraped the toe of my boot. I'm too old for this.

**6 March**

Clive is back, looking very sleepy. I don't ask for the details, but it seems a good time was had by all.

A yoga friend shares a picture on Facebook of a very worthy vegan dish that prompts the question, 'Have you eaten that, or are you just going to?'

**7 March**

A friend confides that her newly retired husband is trying her patience. She tells me, 'Every morning, he wants to know what we're going to do that day. It's like living with a child.' I reassure her that this is normal and say that it took some doing to wean Clive off the idea that every shopping trip would inevitably end in coffee and Danish pastries.

**8 March**
Sam introduces Clive to the wonders of Magic: The Gathering, which is apparently some sort of collectable card game. When I ask if it's like Top Trumps for grown-ups they give me withering looks. Apparently it's nothing like that. I don't know why this feels so much worse that if they were playing bridge, but it does, and that says more about me than it does them. Clive has also reinstalled Pokémon Go on his phone and recent walks have been interrupted by us having to stop while he catches a Jigglypuff or 'levels up', whatever that might mean.

In the evening, one of Clive's former colleagues calls round for a chat. There are rumblings of discontent in certain quarters at work, so he has turned to Clive for some advice, given that he was the Union rep. I wonder if this might escalate. Am I to expect a procession of disgruntled workers seeking wisdom from the Sage on the Hill?

**9 March**
The diet isn't going very well. All that has happened is that we are able to be 'good' during the week, but then weaken at the weekend – and yes, I mean mostly me.

Clive has developed an unexpected fondness for salad, although the addition of pungent pickles has had me reaching for the joss sticks on more than one occasion. Today, though, the weather has turned cold and there's nothing for it: flapjack and biscuits are on the menu, tempered only by a virtuous pea-based curry. Let's gloss over the stack of homemade naan bread.

Then we watch *Dead Pool 2*. You may remember my introduction to this film franchise back in June; this one is in similar vein. It's very sweary, but if you have to watch a superhero film – and it seems I do – it might as well be this one, which is very tongue in cheek, well written and acted, and only slightly too long compared to, say, *The Dark Knight*, which is 152 minutes too long.

## 10 March

We take a walk, going the long way round to town simply to clock up a few miles. We don't take any money, because of our aversion to shopping on a Sunday. I remember the general outcry when the law was changed to extend trading hours to outlets other than little corner shops where you'd go to buy a *Sunday Express*, a pint of milk and a packet of rollups. Now we are indignant if somewhere is closed for a few hours.

## 11 March

The washing-machine man has been back, because the replacement machine delivered just three weeks ago is refusing to drain. He is surprisingly obliging, twiddles a few things and goes away, leaving us happy. Then the gas man comes to service the boiler. Meanwhile, Clive takes his car to the garage for its service and MOT, and this is all before 11 o'clock.

I'm not in the mood for work at all, but soldier on and manage to achieve everything on the agenda for the day. This means we are both sufficiently pleased with ourselves to have a glass of wine with our evening meal, which is most unusual for a Monday.

## 12 March

Clive has just brought me a small glass of something to test. I sniff it tentatively. Sprout water? Dregs from the washing-machine? Honestly, I couldn't tell if it was beer or wine, or something else entirely. When one of our boys was very little, he accidentally took a sip of his father's whisky, after which he declared. 'Yuk! I need to lick the carpet to take the taste away.' I now know how he felt.

On the radio, *You and Yours* has a cheery phone-in edition asking people how they are preparing for Brexit. Most Radio 4 listeners seem to be stockpiling food; one caller runs a company selling survival kits, which seems a little extreme even for Middle England. One of my yoga students has told me her biggest concern is having to buy English wine, rather than French. First world problems. This evening, MPs reject Theresa May's Brexit deal for a second time by a majority of 149. What next, I wonder. The BBC website has a helpful flowchart of how this might all play out and it seems there is a slim chance that we could stay in the EU after all. Enough, now.

## 13 March

Chief project for today is, apparently, to clean out the fish tank. It's strange how something that used to take an hour after work is now scheduled to take half a day. This task has to be put on hold, however, because the washing-machine is leaking. Yes, the new washing-machine that the man came out to two days ago.

Clive digs out his workman's jeans and a manly wrench and sets to dismantling the pipework. There is only one way this can end: with much swearing followed by a trip to the plumber's merchant in town, an emporium guaranteed to have anything you need, be it flux paste, Plumbers Mait or a straight coupler (oo-er). Needless to say, they don't have the right size of washer for Clive and he has to do what he calls a jury-rig and I call a bodge job. There is more swearing.

The fish still cannot see out of their tank.

## 14 March

Another funeral today for Clive to attend. Let's not dwell.

This afternoon I go to give blood, a process that usually passes without incident. Today, though, having donated a pint of my finest O+ and walked across the hall to claim my cup of tea and Penguin reward, I realise that my forearm is scarlet and the plaster on my arm is dripping. Two of the care team leap into action and usher me into a chair, while another brings out the biohazard signs and wetwipes. I feel fine, but am alarmed at the amount of blood that I now see has trailed all the way across the floor and has also soaked into my scarf and is running all down my leg and half a bootful. Eventually, it stops and I am hosed down. Most embarrassing.

## 15 March

The fish tank is cleaned out and aquatic order restored.

After an uneventful day, we sally forth to the Derngate to see Bernie Keith. I should explain that Bernie is a presenter on BBC Radio Northampton and is a proper character, to put it mildly. He has a huge and well-deserved following and an encyclopaedic knowledge of rock 'n' roll. His tone is cheeky and irreverent, but he is never cruel. I am a huge fan. He is also a comedy performer. Clive isn't sure if he wants to go or not, fearing that the audience will be made up largely of women of a certain age and drag queens, though why he should be scared of either of those I don't know. He needn't have worried. There were certainly plenty of the former – I didn't spot any of the latter – but the crowd was a good male/female mix and there were even quite a few under-fifties there. It was a brilliant night.

**16 March**

The wind hasn't let up all week, but there are jobs to be done in the garden. I watch through the window as Clive takes a sledgehammer to a couple of the old fence panels we removed that are now on their way to the dustbin. He doesn't know I'm watching as he takes a particularly satisfying swing, then raises his hands aloft in victory. I return to my own business, but when I look up again he is standing on the other side of the glass, holding his drill like a rifle and pointing it straight at me. Oh dear.

**17 March**

I'm starting to feel guilty about my lack of physical contact with my family up north. Texts and phone calls are all very well, but I need to see them, so we set off up the M1 to Staffordshire. Clive earns himself a gold star by delivering tubs of gingerbread to Mum and to my two brothers' families, along with a couple of bottles of home brew each. This means he can sit in the corner behind the sports section of the newspaper guilt free while Mum and I do battle over world affairs and tackle the cryptic crossword. She tells me she is thinking of dropping out of her ukulele group because she hasn't got time to go. Honestly, she is a powerhouse.

We reward ourselves this evening with a Dominos pizza, the first since 31 May. It is absolutely delicious.

## 18 March

I don't know how this has happened, but Clive has accumulated three pairs of gardening shoes, by which I mean stinky old trainers that he won't let me throw away. This morning he is moving seedlings out of the house and into the greenhouse, so he is tidying up, which is when I notice the footwear mountain. I casually mention that perhaps it might be time to let go of one of the pairs, but he looks at me as though I've suggested selling one of our sons.

'But I *need* them,' he says. 'These are for summer, these are for winter and these are for just in case.'

I stand my ground, however, and manage to prise the oldest pair from his grasp and hold them at arm's length as I despatch them to the dustbin.

## 19 March

A new community website has caught Clive's eye. It is a sort of cross between Freecycle and eBay and yesterday he bagged himself a couple of demijohns and a box of random brewing bits. I'm fine with this. What I'm not so keen on is his scrolling through today to see what else is on offer.

'Oh, look at this,' he says. 'There a whole stack of model railway stuff here. I could buy it and sell it on. It's only £100.'

There are two things to note here. First, he knows nothing about model railways, a fact he vehemently disputes when I point this out. Second, that's a curious use of the word 'only'. Last time I checked, £100 was a lot of money. I decide not to start a row and instead hope that common sense will prevail.

**20 March**
Great excitement today, when another Peter Rabbit coin arrives to add to the collection. They are very pretty, but I'm starting to wonder how many is enough. However, Clive has had a strenuous couple of days, so I suppose he deserves a treat.

Spring has definitely sprung, so he's been up at the allotment emptying the compost bin, riddling the contents and bagging it up. Then he moved the contents of the second bin into the now empty first one and put a layer of shredded paper in the bottom of the second one. Are you still with me? Building a successful compost bin is systematic and systemic. You can't just shove any old rubbish in – oh no. There are protocols to follow that involve layering the correct mix of green and brown waste, and regular turning of the contents to ensure a decent product in the end. I'm happy to leave this task to him; it sounds far too much like hard work. We also have a couple of compost bins at home that I'm allowed to add to. This basically means wrapping vegetable peelings in newspaper and adding them to the mix or putting used tea leaves in, which I can just about manage without causing any lasting damage to the mix.

## 21 March

Some of the burgeoning tomato seedlings are ready to be potted on, but first there is mustard to be made. Yes, that's right, that condiment you can buy from any supermarket for less than £1. Ah, but this is special mustard; this is Beer Mustard. Of course it is. The recipe calls for 350g of mustard seeds, half black and half yellow. Clive has been online and ordered a kilo of each, Lord knows why.

Meanwhile in the real world, as Theresa May goes to Brussels to ask the EU for a delay to next Friday's Brexit date, an online petition calling for her to cancel the whole thing by revoking Article 50 passes a million signatures. Not surprisingly, the website crashes.

## 22 March

My cafetière has been commandeered. Clive 'really needs it' to make a hop tea to add to the ailing batch of beer. Now, I'm all in favour of a cuppa when the spirits need lifting, but I draw the line at this. I am overruled.

Brexit is to be delayed. I can't bring myself to go into details here – and anyway by the time you're reading this it will all have been resolved and we shall be looking back on these crazy times, laughing and saying, 'What were we thinking!'

## 23 March

We're at the Arts Centre again this evening with Terri and Russell to hear musical duo Ward & Parker, supported by our pal Kenneth J Nash. Terri and I really enjoy it, Russell has spent the previous week away in France on a school trip with 80 teenagers and is understandably too tired to express much of an opinion. Clive hates it. I really wonder about him sometimes.

## 24 March

I spend a large part of today in Northampton. I am a judge at the Open Stage Performance Awards, watching youngsters from 2 to 18 singing, dancing and acting. I've done this before and it is the most amazing thing to be involved in. I say 'judge', but that's not really the right word, because what myself and the other judge Jules (see 8 December) do is sit there open-mouthed at the talent and sheer bravery of everyone who takes part. The event is really to get the participants used to how it feels to perform to an audience. No one is forced to do it and there is no *X Factor*-style assassination.

Sam joins us for dinner, then we slump on the sofa in front of *Mad Men*. All in all, a satisfactory day.

## 25 March

The sun is out, so on a whim we head for the coast. Unfortunately, our nearest bit of coast is Hunstanton, which in the summer is like one of Dante's infernal circles. However, out of season and with virtually everything closed, there is space to appreciate how pretty the little town is and of course the sea is there, waiting to recharge our batteries. We have a lovely walk, including taking in Hunstanton's extraordinary cliff. Clive is in his element, explaining how the very clearly defined strands of rock signify a catastrophic event: perhaps a sudden change in temperature or sea level. Whatever caused it, it is very impressive and I am moved to take a photo and post it on Facebook with the simple comment: 'Skiving.' On a whim, we call in at the Sea Life Centre and stroke a starfish. We agree, this is a great day to be retired/self-employed.

## 26 March

It's Tuesday, but because of yesterday's adventure it feels like Monday. An awful incident at the school where I usually teach on Tuesday means the class has to be cancelled, throwing me even further out of balance. In the afternoon I take a screen break and walk up to the allotment to see how Clive is getting on. I have to say he is doing great work up there and it's starting to look very promising.

Clive, though, is in reflective mood. He says, 'I keep looking over at Malcolm's plot. I can't get my head around the fact that I shan't see him again.'

## 27 March

Something is happening in parliament today. The phrase 'indicative vote' is being bandied about, though I'm not convinced anyone knows what it really means. Then later in the day the PM promises to quit if her deal is approved. I'm not sure how this will help.

Fortunately, I have my dancetheatre session this evening to take my mind off everything. I come home refreshed in mind and well and truly stretched in body. Clive follows me in, clutching a Dove toiletries gift set that he has won in a raffle. He has been to his archaeology group meeting for a talk on Viking weaving. He wasn't looking forward to it, but says actually it was fascinating and he even had a go at spinning. This is why so far we haven't run out of things to say to each other.

## 28 March

A friend calls in for coffee and we discuss the feasibility of her moving house. I relate the conversation to Clive and of course this makes us think about our own situation. He would like to move to the coast, but I worry about leaving behind everyone I know. How would we (by which I mean I) manage without the support network we have built up over the 30-something years we've been in Kettering? What if we moved to Northumberland and one of us died? It's being so cheerful that keeps me going.

## 29 March

With Clive's birthday coming up, we skive off again to find him a present. We head for Peterborough, which has lovely limestone paving in its shopping centre that always pleases us. The shopping isn't all that successful, but we have a nice time pootling about.

What sets us off in a good mood is going into John Lewis, not to buy anything, but to wander around the kitchen section. It's hilarious. There are so many ridiculous gadgets on sale for stupid prices. For £10 you can buy a giant pencil sharpener for peeling carrots, or some little hairnets to protect the cut surface of a lemon, should putting it upside-down on a plate be beyond you. For £12 you can buy tongs for extracting a boiled egg from a pan, in case you don't have any spoons. Or you could go wild and for £18 treat yourself to a self-tapping sieve. Say, what? Best of all, buy a JosephJoseph GoAvocado tool, which 'cuts, de-stones and slices'. What, like a knife? We also see an enormous, gleaming coffee-making machine. I'm sorry, but if you've got £2,000 to spend on making a cappuccino you have too much money.

We stop for a drink. We have to move tables when the one next to us is occupied by a couple who encourage a yappy little dog up on to their stretch of the communal seating. I growl.

There is some lovely artwork on the walls, which I gaze at while Clive, somewhat inevitably, pops to the Gents. When he comes back he picks up his jacket from the back of his chair and walks off, notwithstanding that I'm still sitting there drinking my tea. It's only when he reaches the door that he looks round to see where I am. I make a mental note to start researching care homes.

**30 March**

The approaching end of yet another month prompts reflection. Clive is loving retirement most of the time, but from where I'm sitting he doesn't seem to have any structure to his days. I don't know if this bothers him or not, but there are certainly times when it bothers me. I suppose that having spent all those years being told what to do, it must be lovely to be able please himself, to get up when he wakes and to potter if there's nothing specific on the agenda. I don't want him to get too comfortable, though, because comfy is only a couple of steps away from stationary.

On the other hand, he has been persuaded to stand for the position of Chairman of the local Allotment Society. I say persuaded: I mean badgered. I'm sure he'll be good at it, but mostly I'm thinking that this will be another reason for him to get out and about a bit.

**31 March**

It's Mothering Sunday. Pedants will be pleased to note I refused to call it Mother's Day – and shouldn't that be Mothers' Day anyway, since we're honouring all of them, not just the one? The clan gathers in the afternoon and we have a drop of Bucks Fizz to mark the day. There is, of course, a balloon. Clive excels in the kitchen again, producing the most amazing homemade pizza.

# APRIL

## 1 April

I receive a text from the blood people to say the effusive donation I made a couple of weeks ago has been issued to Royal Surrey Hospital. I wonder who's got it.

It's a glorious spring day and Clive goes off to the plot with a song in his heart and more onion sets in his bag. He has a good day, but manages to wear himself out. Poor old thing.

## 2 April

After the energetic day he had yesterday, Clive takes it easy today, because, as he points out, he can. I try not to tut. Is this the pattern now? One busy day, followed by one day to recover? He does manage to go to B&Q to buy some compost. He gets all the way to the checkout and has had everything scanned before he realises he has left his wallet in his other jacket. He comes home empty-handed.

## 3 April

Clive's birthday today, so I treat him to bacon and black pudding for breakfast. Yes, I, the vegetarian, start the day over a pan of dead pig. Greater love... When he shows me some lovely comments on Facebook, I notice his profile still shows him as employed by his old firm.

'Yes,' he says. 'I should probably change that,' but he doesn't.

Is he still hedging his bets?

## 4 April

Clive is caught browsing the internet for model railway starter sets. Later that same day, he discovers that the Bluetooth speaker he received as a present yesterday has a button on it that turns it into an electronic drum kit. It is a trying day.

## 5 April

While I spend 90 minutes in the optician's, Clive does a little gentle dusting before being distracted by the prospect of brewing. He takes a long hard look at the dodgy beer that he had to filter and transfer to a different vessel, and decides there's nothing else for it, it will have to go. Considering that this is his first real failure, I don't think this is too much of a drama. I am wrong. A lengthy trawl through advice given on the online forums leads him to the conclusion that not only will the beer have to go, but also everything it has touched must be cleansed with caustic soda. This seems a bit drastic to me and I venture to suggest that it might be better to cut his losses and just buy some new kit. He gives me a scornful look.

For respite, he tackles one of his pension providers for an update on what he needs to do to withdraw some funds. The company has already sent him a pack of bumf (whatever happened to the paperless society?) that he was advised to read before ringing them. He has done this, but has to endure another lengthy conversation and will be sent yet more forms before he can get his hands on what is, after all, his money.

An evening of comedy at the Lighthouse with Rachel Parris restores our mood.

## 6 April

There's golf today, so I have the house to myself. I immerse myself in another Jack Reacher novel until

Clive returns victorious, but only just. He's had a mare of a game and is not best pleased with himself.

Again, comedy comes to the rescue: this time Tony Law at the Arts Centre. He is very, very strange.

## 7 April

It's a misty, murky morning, but we've promised ourselves a walk so we set off to follow a circular route on the edge of Rutland Water. It's rather dull, because it's such a flat county and the weather doesn't help. Nevertheless, Clive stops every now and then to drop to his knees and examine a bit of rock through his new lens. He is particularly pleased to find some granite chippings, which he concludes must have been imported by the farmer to add substance to the track on which we are walking. I prefer to think that some prankster brought them with him from, say, Bodmin and dropped them here on purpose to confuse amateur geologists.

As we turn the last corner before reaching the village where we parked our car, we are startled to see a dead rabbit wedged between the branches of a tree. Another prankster, or a predator saving a snack for later?

## 8 April

There is much digging and planting to be done today, so I have a whole day of uninterrupted work. Not very interesting and certainly not very amusing, but at least it was profitable.

## 9 April

Yesterday's toil is evidenced in Clive's buttocks this morning. He walks downstairs without bending his knees and each step is accompanied by either an 'Ooh' or an 'Aargh'. He is, of course, that little bit older than me, I remind him, smugly. Once he gets going he fills his day and the house with the smell of silage, as he tackles another SMaSH brew. Joe pops in for a sandwich at lunchtime and has to go to the back of the house to eat it, as the stench in the kitchen proves too much for him.

Clive's range of movement improves as the day wears on, and he is able to go to the meeting that confirms him as Chairman of Kettering Allotment Society. When Sam learns of his father's elevation, he suggests there should be a Turnip Tax, some sort of feudal system in which other gardeners should proffer a vegetable-based offering to secure their tenancy.

## 10 April

While I hurtle towards a copy deadline, Clive joins me in the back room to tackle a mountain of paperwork that he has accumulated. When I say 'paperwork', I really mean electronic clutter. He has the habit of reading emails but then not taking any action, which means he ends up with dozens waiting for attention, some of which have been contradicted by later communications by the time he gets to them, meaning he has to do the same job at least twice. It's not my problem, but he's there in my peripheral vision, and there's quite a lot of tutting and sighing. At one point when I leave the room and go upstairs, I can hear him swearing at his computer even though I'm on the landing.

That evening, some friends ask me, 'How are things, really?' Perhaps I look pale. I consider telling them what a frustrating day I've had, but realise that it would sound petty. Instead, I smile and say, 'It's mostly good, thanks. At least, not as bad as I feared it would be when Clive first retired.' The truth, if not the whole truth.

**11 April**

Cleaning out the pockets of his allotment trousers, Clive proudly brings forth a small but perfectly formed brachiopod that he found while planting his leeks. It's barely 1cm across its widest part and is rather beautiful. He is ridiculously pleased with it.

**12 April**

It's our wedding anniversary today. We are long past the stage of exchanging cards and gifts, but plan to go to Derbyshire for a walk. In the event, the weather isn't particularly encouraging and I have lots of work to do in a very short time, so while I crack on with that Clive goes to – yes, you've guessed – the allotment. We toy with the idea of a fancy dinner out, but in the end settle for fish and chips, which always feels rather naughty and is hence extremely satisfying. So no oysters and champagne, but after 39 years what can you expect?

## 13 April

Somewhat against my better judgement, I go to the car showroom to look at the new Fiesta, having been promised the deal of a lifetime by the eager young pup on the phone. To be honest, it doesn't look all that different to me, but it does have a sort of floating computer screen in the centre of the dashboard, a warning light on the wing mirror to warn of vehicles in the blind spot, the option to vibrate the steering wheel should the car wander out of its lane, and the engine switches off in a traffic jam. These are all touted as Good Things.

Later, Clive goes golfing with his holiday mates and comes back with a very red face. I mention sun cream. He scowls at me.

## 14 April

We go off in different directions today, me to do something arty with my dancetheatre pals, Clive to play golf again. We both come home with aching legs.

Sitting on the sofa watching TV later, Clive becomes aware of a breeze around his nethers. When he stands up he discovers a massive rip in his best golfing trousers, but has no recollection of it appearing. Certainly it wasn't there when he left home. Does this mean he played 18 holes with his pants on show? I despair. He's not safe out on his own.

## 15 April

There is consternation this morning, because it looks as though some of our tomato seedlings might have a touch of sunburn. It's probably not fatal, but there is much chin-stroking. There's better news from the allotment, though, where everything Clive has planted so far seems to have taken.

I am out in the evening, chatting on local radio about public speaking. This has been arranged at short notice, so I suspect I wasn't first choice. However, I have no pride, so off I trot. This means I'm not at home to witness the latest instalment of the Great Golf Holiday Planning Process. At least they've started planning a bit earlier than last time, but honestly, you'd think they were preparing to go across the Kalahari on a skateboard, rather than to Wales in a 4x4. To my mind, they're making it unnecessarily complicated, but it's not really my problem. I feign interest in all the machinations on my return, but offer no opinion, just some soothing noises.

## 16 April

This morning's news bulletins are full of the story that Notre Dame caught fire last night. Of course, the conspiracy theorists are having a field day, pointing out that it was very convenient that the most valuable statues had been removed the day before 'for cleaning'. Paris has grand plans for its renovation, which is pleasing some people and making others cross, because of the amount of money involved. I don't care much either way.

This evening, while I don't know for sure, I suspect that all those text messages Clive receives while we are watching TV are from his golf pals. Every time he responds to the call of the Samsung Siren, he tuts loudly before typing something in reply with unnecessary force. I am on the verge of taking over and booking the damned holiday myself.

## 17 April

It's time for the annual battle over the forget-me-nots. I think these tiny blue flowers are lovely and should be cherished; Clive thinks they're weeds and should be uprooted. He is wrong, of course, and I will not be moved on this. As he gets out the mower to give the lawn a pre-Easter trim, I remind him not to cull the wildflowers, then I rush out to pick some daisies before they all lose their heads. He draws the line at preserving the dandelions, despite my protestations that the bees love them and therefore we should leave them. *He* won't be moved on this. Marriage is all about compromise, apparently.

## 18 April

It's all a bit tetchy at the moment. With a game of golf planned for this afternoon, Clive doesn't think it's worth starting anything this morning. I make a big show of being very busy. It's not his fault, of course. He has plenty of time to do stuff, so naturally doesn't hurtle around, but a bit more oomph wouldn't go amiss.

The much anticipated David Attenborough programme *Climate Change: The Facts* is on TV this evening, which we feel obliged to watch. It is very disappointing. For one thing, three-quarters of it is devoted to shots of sad-faced animals against a swell of emotive music. Where is the science? And while we all know that Mr A can do no wrong, he is just a TV presenter, not a messenger from the Almighty. What really bugged me, though, was the implication that it's all our fault: that we buy too much, travel too far and waste too much food. Well, I'm sorry, but as long as MPs are being driven everywhere in gas-guzzlers, I don't think my taking the cellophane off window envelopes before I recycle them is going to make much difference. The government needs to step up.

Anyway, we both get in a bit of a lather about the programme. Clive reminds me that he has a degree in Natural Science and knows that these climatic cycles are natural. He keeps telling me that Earth will survive, even if humans don't. I retort that this will be small comfort to the people of East Anglia when their homes fall into the sea, which he counters with, 'Well, it shouldn't be there anyway. It's reclaimed land.'

Tempers and nostrils flaring, we decide we'd better not talk about it anymore.

## 19 April

Another grumpy day, but we have a trip to the theatre tonight to see Ibsen's *Ghosts*, which is very good, if a bit long. Yes: theatre on Good Friday. I didn't know that was allowed.

We notice that our radiators are getting hot, even though the heating is switched off. A gas man will be summoned in the morning.

## 20 April

The weather is really hotting up, but I slap on the sun cream and go out with the dancetheatre group to film a performance in various locations around Corby. (Should you be interested, Google 'Pina Bausch Nelken Line', for it was that.)

On my return, I catch Clive Googling model railway ephemera, including something called Track Magic. One can only wonder. There is apparently to be a huge gathering of likeminded souls somewhere nearby over the summer. I murmur something noncommittal, because I know if I express any reservations he will be even more determined to attend.

## 21 April

It's Easter Sunday and the sun is out. We spend the day pottering at home. The 'kids' come over for a drink and a natter. They are very easy to be around. Joe and Caitlin are full of plans for their new home, especially her. It's lovely to bask in the glow of their youthful enthusiasm. Clive has been roped into driving the van for moving day. It amuses me how much he is looking forward to this. Being in charge of a Transit for a day is right up there with firing up the barbeque on the manliness scale. I offer to help with the cleaning. Did someone say gender stereotyping?

## 22 April

After the lethargy of yesterday, we head off into the Northamptonshire wilderness for a walk. Whether it is the lack of distraction or the fact that we are side by side, rather than face to face, but we often thrash out issues while we're tramping in the countryside. So it is today. We are both aware that there's been a lot of sniping over the last few days, and I eventually confess that he is driving me crazy at the moment, though I also say it's because I'm overreacting and envious of his freedom to do nothing, should he choose to.

When, in return, I ask him what I'm doing that's annoying him, he says, 'Nothing. I love you just the way you are.'

I feel terrible.

## 23 April

The gas engineer who was promised 'sometime between 8am and 1pm' does not appear. When I ring to enquire as to his whereabouts, I am told that there is no record of the appointment on the British Gas system. I am not best pleased. Apparently, the problem is something to do with a code number. As I point out in my best clipped tone, this matters not to me. I simply want an engineer to come out without further delay. I am put on hold. I've done my share of telesales work and I know that this means he's now telling his colleagues that he has a grumpy old bag on the phone. I also suspect that if you ask to speak to a supervisor, all that happens is that the agent passes the phone to a nearby person of the same rank and with just the same level of power, or lack of it. After half an hour, I am eventually told that someone will come round tomorrow between 12 and 2.

Seeking solace in nature, I throw some grapes that are past their best out on to the lawn and watch as two magpies chase them around for a while before it finally dawns on them how to pick them up. Once they have them grasped in their pointy beaks they sit for a moment, as if wondering what on earth to do next.

## 24 April

Clive has declared himself bankrupt.

Not on purpose, I hasten to add, but accidentally. He filled in a form to claim another chunk from the pension pot and ticked the wrong box. He only discovered this when he rang the company to see what the delay was. They had been checking into his background and were mystified to find no record of profligacy. Not surprising, really. So it's back to square one with a new form and perhaps a new pair of glasses.

Speaking of glasses, I have some new specs. They make me look like Velma from *Scooby-Doo*.

Oh, by the way, the gas man came!

## 25 April

Clive sets up camp in the back garden with bags of compost and a mountain of plant pots. By the end of the day he has sown 13 courgette seeds. Not unreasonable, you might think – but each plant is likely to yield at least one fruit a day for up to two months. That's potentially 780 courgettes. He's also started off 10 butternut squash (that's up to 40 fruit) and 12 Crown Prince pumpkins (at least two fruit per plant). Oh, and 22 sweetcorn plants. I remind him that there are only two of us to feed.

## 26 April

Clive wonders if the washing-machine is playing up again, because his favourite jumper has shrunk. Yes, I say, maybe.

## 27 April

I come home this afternoon from playing in a ukulele concert to find the house filled with the smell of homemade oat biscuits. There goes the diet, then, but boy, they're worth the sacrifice.

## 28 April
There are many around us who are struggling with various challenges at the moment. This, and the cheery reminder by some random post on Facebook that 'Many who will die this morning had plans for this evening', encourages us to set out for Rutland Water to make the most of the day, just in case. It's cool, but bright, which makes for perfect walking. We pause for a breather on a bench overlooking the reservoir and watch as three fluffy ducklings try out some manoeuvres in front of us, then disappear around the bend out of sight. Five minutes later a swan appears in the other direction.

'Blimey,' says Clive, 'that was a quick transformation.'

Further down the path, a fox dashes out in front of us in hot pursuit of something only he can see. There are rabbits and lambs, and the most incredible expanse of bluebells. It's good to be alive.

## 29 April
Invigorated by yesterday, we both hit the ground running today. I have a new yoga client and my first session goes well.

Clive returns from the allotment red-faced from the sun and absolutely filthy. He's had a good day. He is particularly pleased that the newly planted asparagus shows signs of life. As he puts it: 'Tricky blighter, asparagus.' It will be three years before we can eat any spears, if we can keep it alive that long.

**30 April**
With a lull in my workload, I treat myself to a long walk that includes a detour to the allotment. I arrive to see Clive scratching his head and scowling at the mower.

I hear him say, 'What's wrong with you now? Bloody machine!'

His diagnosis is that it's overheated, and sure enough after a half-hour breather it starts first time. Reminds me of someone. I pick the only two rhubarb stems to stew for tea.

In the evening we go to the Derngate to see *Paul Merton's Impro Chums*, which is like *Whose Line Is It Anyway* off the telly, but I suspect the name has had to be changed for copyright reasons. When the interval arrives, we are amused to see the couple in front of us produce a mini coolbag from which they withdraw two chocolate eclairs on paper plates. There are some very strange people in this world. We content ourselves with two of Gallone's finest ice-cream tubs. There is a bit of comedy when Clive turns into a supreme juggler as one and then the other tub falls from his hands. There is a moment when it looks as though they and he will land full square in the cream cakes, but he saves his dignity just in time.

# MAY

## 1 May
Facebook is awash with Beltane Blessings.

## 2 May
Clive is continuing to go to Tai Chi every Thursday morning. After having endured him poking a little gentle fun at my Adho Mukha Svanasana all these years (that's Downward Facing Dog, in case you're wondering), I feel no qualms about renaming his

demonstration of 'Catching the sparrow's tail' as 'Tickling the weasel'. I fear the joke is wearing thin.

## 3 May

Great excitement today, as Clive takes receipt of a lorry-load of IBCs to be used at the allotment to catch rainwater. Each one holds 1,000 litres, so should serve the gardeners well. Given the way it rains when I go for a walk this morning, they shouldn't take too long to fill. While I am out, I come across an epic rooks versus squirrel battle in the woods. I think at first a child is being murdered, but then realise it is the poor squirrel jumping from branch to branch while the evil birds gang up on it. I watch until it finally escapes and disappears into the distance.

The results of yesterday's local elections are coming through and it looks as though the Lib Dems are the only winners, if you can call them that. The Tories in particular suffered several defeats. It does seem a shame that the poor local councillors who (I'll give them the benefit of the doubt) work hard for their communities have to bear the brunt of Brexit fallout. We didn't vote here. Our county is to be phased out and replaced with a Unitary Authority. What could possibly go wrong?

## May The Fourth

OK, I get it – Star Wars Day. Ha-ha, very funny. It's a great excuse for people old enough to know better to dress up as their favourite characters. Is it mean-spirited of me to suggest that if you were of an age to appreciate Princess Leia at the time the first film came out, you're probably too old to squeeze into her costume now?

Never mind all that, though. Today Clive goes off to fetch the Transit he has reserved to help Joe and Caitlin move house in the morning. All booked, deposit paid, ID documents at the ready. Except...

I get a frantic phone call from him asking for his National Insurance number, which I'm able to locate with ease, because I'm a filing demon. Ten minutes later there's another phone call from him, not so much frantic as furious now, saying that the website that the hire firm uses to check NI references is down, so they won't let him have the van. There's nothing to be done, so he stomps home, which is mostly uphill, at a ridiculous rage-fuelled pace. When he comes through the front door I'm sure he's about to have a stroke, because his face is the colour of freshly boiled beetroot and he can hardly speak, such is the battle for breath.

The next hour is tense, to put it mildly. This being a Bank Holiday weekend, no other hire places are open. I throw out an appeal for help on Facebook, where a dear friend in Wales offers to drive up. Touched as I am by what I know is a genuine offer of help, it seems a little extreme. I ring Debs for advice and she steps into the breach. Without missing a beat, she offers to borrow her son-in-law's truck and drive it for us. That woman is a diamond.

## 5 May

Moving day goes pretty well, in the end. There is a little bit of discreet rivalry between the dads over who is the more useful, but I manage to keep my control freakery at bay. As far as I'm aware no one cries. The only breakage is a single plate (well done, Clive). Again, we envy Joe and Caitlin their youthful optimism. As protective parents, we can see little flaws in their place, but they are happy simply to be in their new home. Ain't love grand?

## 6 May

After the stress of the last couple of days, a walk is very much on the agenda for this morning. We take a detour to the allotment (obviously), where Clive points out his IBC array. We chat with a few folk. There are rumblings of discontent over the provision of water. There are only three taps for the whole field, which some folk aren't happy with. Of course, if everyone had an IBC, we wouldn't need the taps.

## 7 May

I have a new car. It is another red Fiesta, but has an incredible array of technological delights. I can control my phone from my car and my car from my phone. I can ask the radio to find the nearest petrol station and the i-Pad-style screen helpfully points out the speed limit. It has lane assist, tracking control and lights that come on without me having to lift a finger. It's all very clever. This doesn't stop me having three goes at reversing into a space in the theatre car park this evening, but that's down to my brain, not the car's.

We're at the theatre to see *Rock of Ages*, the campest, cheesiest, cheekiest, rockiest musical extravaganza we've ever witnessed. The celeb turn in the role of baddy is Anthony Costa, him out of Blue, who turns out to have a surprisingly good voice (no offence, Tone), but it's the rest of the cast that shine. The audience is comprised mostly of tubby old men and women in clothes that are a bit too tight, trying to relive their glory days. We include ourselves in that bracket. There's nothing quite like a thousand pensioners rocking out to 'Don't Stop Believing'. It does your heart good. It was a brilliant end to a pretty good day.

**8 May**
On a pouring wet day, there's only one thing for it: brewing. My friend Elaine is back from New Zealand and is calling in for a catch-up, so I'm slightly concerned that the smell of warm barley might be rather off-putting. Indignant at the thought, Clive makes a big show of opening all the windows. In the event, Elaine isn't at all bothered and the 'quick cuppa' takes us three hours.

**9 May**
Clive sets off in the rain to meet his geology chums to do another survey of local rocks. Yes, I know there's

more to it than this, but you get the idea. He comes home six hours later having been soaked to the skin and then dry several times. On the other hand, there was a bacon and sausage bap at lunchtime, so it wasn't all bad.

I'm so pleased that he's finally making use of his OU degree. He's always thought of himself as not particularly academic, but I beg to differ. Not only has he studied natural sciences, but he can also remember what he's learned, so now that the lid has been taken off he's rediscovering his passion for the subject. Having tried various groups over the last nearly 12 months, it feels as though he's at last starting to settle in to a new routine that involves some new enterprises, like the Tai Chi, but also a return to things he hasn't had time to do for years. Is this, the secret to a happy retirement?

**10 May**
Joe and Clive tackle the last part of clearing Joe's old house with many trips to the tip. They work hard, so Clive deserves the evening's entertaining, which is a tour of the Pot Belly Brewery. There are five couples in our party and we have a great time, with just the right amount of beer, a fish and chip supper, a couple of games of pool and lots of laughter. The uphill walk home in a light drizzle clears our heads.

**11 May**
The world of online gaming is one I'm happy to know little about, and I tell myself that it's mostly harmless at

the level Clive indulges. He only downloads the free games and doesn't buy extra costumes or supplies of food and medicine for his characters. It is a bit rum, though. I know that each player uses an alias, and I'm not sure if I'm amused or perturbed to find Clive has been playing with 'Trixie', 'Mindsweeper' (not a typo) and 'Grunge Boy'. Clive's own nom de guerre is such that it has been abbreviated to 'Rock'. I ask him if this is deliberate. He says, 'Of course not – it never occurred to me. It is quite cool, though.' Honestly. Boys.

This evening there's nothing on the telly, so on a whim we venture out to hear a tribute to Tony Hancock. Let's just say it wasn't the best thing we've ever been to.

## 12 May

Clive goes golfing and I try to have a day off, but I can't decide what to do, so I spent the day nearly doing this and that, but mostly sighing. Joe and Caitlin pop in briefly and it dawns on me that I'm in full-on scruff mode and I feel embarrassed, dowdy and old. Clive has a roast chicken for his tea (not a whole one – not quite) and I have some leftover curry, which I can't be bothered to reheat, so deep is my grump. The evening is saved when Clive suggests we watch a film, *Sully*, about the pilot who brought his plane down on the Hudson. It's so realistic that we both brace when the captain orders the passengers to prepare for a bumpy landing. It stars Tom Hanks in the title role; has that man ever made a bad film?

## 13 May

Broad beans are curious things. You can plant a whole row from the same packet and only half of them will germinate. I walk up to see Clive at the allotment and catch him scratching his head at this leguminous letdown, where an erratic array of tiny shoots are appearing along the bed. I point out that there are only two of us and the 30 or so that have taken will probably be more than adequate for our needs; we still have some of last year's in the freezer, after all. This is scant consolation. On the other hand, the onions are already nearly waist high.

We are distracted by the sight of a pall of black smoke over the town in the distance. Later we learn that this is the demise of a bedding centre that has been there as long as anyone can remember and, like so many businesses around here, occupies a former shoe factory that was originally built in the 19th century, right in the middle of the residential area from where it drew its workers. The three-storey building has gone up like a tinder box. Residents are evacuated and the nearby primary school is closed for the rest of the day. No one is hurt, and the rumour that an adjacent house is also lost turns out to be false, but it's a sad day for the town.

**14 May**

My day begins with the news that I shall not after all be required to teach meditation tomorrow in a local senior school, because it transpires there is no budget. Given the modest amount I've asked for, it occurs to me that they might have been expecting me to do this for love. It is a common misconception that yoga teachers don't need paying, but rather share their knowledge for the joy of spreading the message. Oh well. Namaste.

My mood is lifted, however, when I realise that we do after all have tomtits in the nesting box outside my window. I spend far too long with my head craned at an awkward angle so I can watch their comings and goings. In other ornithological news, a flock of baby starlings takes more than a passing interest in the courgette seedlings taking in the sun on the patio. I push the plants back into the compost. Clive need never know.

**15 May**

Clive's words on waking this morning: 'Ooh, buttocks!'

I hope this is only down to too much weeding at the allotment yesterday. Groaning glutes notwithstanding, he does manage to get out of bed, enticed by the prospect of a 'quick nine' later in the day. His mood is further lifted with a neighbour asks him if he can tag along next time he goes up to the allotment. Clive is cock-a-hoop. Then to top it all he wins a bottle of wine in the raffle at an event at the art gallery.

**16 May**

The planned visit to the allotment with our neighbour goes well and Clive returns glowing with pride, bless him. It seems these two retired gents have compared notes on life without paid employment, and one thing Clive shares is that he had hoped for more days out. I'd hoped for this, too, but when the work is there for me I have to do it. Yes, I'm self-employed, so in theory I could say 'Sod it' and set off with my knapsack on my back, but such wanton behaviour would come home to roost when the credit card bill landed.

I'm rather surprised at how bitter and twisted I feel about this. I love my work and realise I'm very lucky not to be spending nine hours a day on my feet in a cold factory taking the innards out of chickens. Even so, today I'd have given anything not to have had to work. Honestly, there's no pleasing some folk.

**17 May**

Clive comes home from Morrisons with everything on the list except the cucumber, declaring, 'They were all just too flaccid.'

**18 May**

We set off for a seven-mile circular walk that takes in local landmark Foxton Locks. It's overcast but mild, and although there is a bit of rain every now and then it doesn't really trouble us. The good thing is that it has deterred most people from venturing out, so everywhere is quiet. There are a lot of stiles along the way, in an entertaining array of designs, some of which momentarily confuse us. With each one, the level of Clive's sound effects increases from a satisfied 'Ah' on landing on the other side, to a full on 'Oof' as he launches himself off the ground. Well, he is five years older than me; I might have mentioned this before. With unerring accuracy, he also manages to stick his hand into bird poo on the top rung with such regularity that I begin to wonder if he's doing it on purpose.

When we reach the locks themselves we lean over the bridge, taking in the view. There is a party of four on the opposite side, but one of them, a gent in blazer and tie, comes over to where we are standing and leans so close to me I can smell his breakfast. I turn my head to nod hello, but he is oblivious. My invisibility cloak is working well today.

**19 May**

The ukulele orchestra has been invited to play at the Mayor's spring fete in a nearby village. Tempted by the prospect of a pint of real ale and a hog roast, Clive tags along. There's lots going on, including dog agility displays, firefighters demonstrating their prowess, funfair rides, charity side shows, WI cakes and, yes, lots of food. An area has been set up with straw bales provided as seating for the anticipated crowd. It's all very *Midsomer Murders* though thankfully without the homicide. As expected, few people actually sit and watch us, but some stand and clap along. All in all, it's a lovely afternoon.

Later, while I recline on the sofa with Jack Reacher, Clive sets about cooking us a meal, his pig-based snack a distant memory. Suddenly, amid the clatter of pots and pans I hear him launch into one of those fully orchestrated sneezing fits I've come to expect, during which he drops a dish from some height into the washing-up bowl and soaks himself in sudsy water.

## 20 May

Another Monday morning dawns and there is much to be done inside and out. We separate to do our various tasks with a cheery 'See you sometime.' There's a lot to be said for days like this, uneventful but peaceful.

## 21 May

Concerns over a little local difficulty that threatens to turn into a full-on plumbing disaster bring Joe to our door with a basket of dirty laundry and a pleading look on his face. It's nice to be wanted. It says a lot for the tedium of my day that this unexpected domestic chore provides a little light relief. Some days I just want to run away and join the circus.

## 22 May

Despite beavering away with a furrowed brow, I clearly don't look busy enough and Clive calls me from the kitchen: 'Can I borrow you for a minute?'

He has covered the floor and most of the work surfaces with old towels and is attempting to decant wine from one demijohn into another with a length of plastic pipe and a little bag of netting that looks like an 18th-century condom.

'I need you to hold this,' he says.

'What?' I say, not unreasonably.

'This!'

I point out that repeating the same word but louder doesn't make it any more comprehensible.

'This! This piece of pipe, obviously! Not like that, lift it up a bit lower!'

This doesn't make sense. He uses his chin to indicate that what he means is hold the pipe a bit lower down and then lift it up. Oh, right. I bite my tongue and do as instructed. I am allowed to return to my desk and the rest of the day passes without incident.

Well, almost. I return from an evening out with friends to find a note: 'Gone to Joe's house.' Oh dear. I fear the worst, plumbing-wise, and so it transpires. There is indeed water in places where there shouldn't be. Dad to the rescue.


**23 May**

The day we've all been waiting for: polling for the European Elections. Most people don't care about this; fewer still understand why we're even bothering, given that we are supposed to be leaving the EU. I'm wondering what isn't being done while all this energy is being expended on Brexit, and yes I know that the MEP vote is, strictly speaking, a different question, but you get my drift. However, a vote is a vote and it's a privilege to be able to use it, so I do. Unlike domestic elections, we have to pick a party rather than an individual.

As I look down the list of options, I realise I'm choosing the least bad one, and wonder if 'None of the above' is viable.

**24 May**

While I'm out in Melton Mowbray with a friend, the news breaks that Theresa May has announced she will be leaving office on 7 June. She can barely hold back the tears, poor old thing.

Closer to home, Clive does battle with HMRC over tax codes and the like. It's something to do with needing a P45 from his pension company, because the Tax Office thinks he was employed by them, even though he clearly wasn't. It's all very wearing.

**25 May**

I have an early class to teach today, and by the time I get home Clive is setting off to the allotment. The 12 pumpkin seeds he sowed earlier have all taken and all been transferred and he needs to check on them. I don't think it will matter if half of them have been taken by rabbits, but I keep this to myself.

**26 May**

Caitlin and Joe call in, the former having returned from a week away with some friends and looking sunkissed and relaxed, the latter relieved to have her home. Sam joins us for some food and is on top form. Sometimes you don't have to do anything to have a good time.

Late in the evening, the results of the European Elections start to come in and Huw Edwards on BBC1 does his best to whip up a bit of enthusiasm. We are not happy with the result.

**27 May**

We take a rather unsatisfactory walk that begins in a very pretty village, but then turns out to be rather dull. We are following a route suggested in a walking magazine, but there is too much of it on the road and the scenery, such as it is, is mostly hidden behind hedges. Then it rains.

Six miles into the seven-mile circuit we are called upon to open a gate into a field and walk straight across it. Unfortunately, there are many cows standing at said gate with their enormous heads all pointing in our direction. As we stand there trying to decide whether or not to venture forth, more cows canter down to join the herd. I've read too many stories about people being trampled underfoot to want to risk it and I'm on the verge of turning round and retracing the entire route. Fortunately, Clive is much more sensible than me. He reminds me that we have both watched a YouTube video called something like 'How to cross a field full of cows without getting killed' and he opens the gate. The cows take a step back and give him the once-over, but then just stand there. Against my better judgement I join him and he's right, of course; the beasts are just curious and when they realise we can offer them nothing in the way of food or entertainment they take no further interest. Nevertheless, my heart is pounding and I don't breathe out until we reach the safety of the other side.

All this means that neither of us is really in the mood for a party, but we've been invited to a gathering at Kezzabelle's house, so we stick some beers in a carrier bag and set off. This turns out to be an excellent decision. Having said we'd only stay for half an hour or so, it is nearly six hours later that we actually stagger back.

## 28 May

The older I get, the tetchier I get. Let's just say that the young gentleman in the car dealership won't cross me again.

Clive is nursing a bit of an injury today. When we were out walking yesterday, he caught his foot on something invisible and performed a rather splendid forward roll down the hill. At the time I just laughed. However, it transpires he landed awkwardly and his wrist took the full force of his bulk and today it is quite painful. I'm such a bad wife.

Worse, I drag him along to a spoken word event in the evening. Actually, I don't drag him as such, because at the party yesterday he seemed very keen to go. Must have been the vegan sausage rolls talking.

**29 May**
There is another indecipherable note in my diary for today: 'Ask by Jean.' Not a clue.

There's an interesting talk at the archaeology group this evening, on the bog bodies of Europe. There are more of them than you might think, and Clive brings home a really interesting leaflet that gives details of where and when they were found, in what condition and the cause of death. Poor old Dätgen Man was discovered in 1959. He was thought to have died in about 150BCE at age 30. I say died: cause of death is given as 'Stabbed three times in the chest and decapitated.' That'll do it.

This talk comes on the day that Clive hears he's been accepted on to an archaeological dig. From Monday he will be spending three weeks on his hands and knees with a trowel, recovering human remains from a Roman cemetery. That's something I never thought I'd see.

**30 May**
I spend today looking back over the past year, rereading the notes I've made. I'm amazed what a long time it seems since last summer and how much I've forgotten,

even though I've written it down. I wonder what else I've let slip from my mind.

## 31 May

So that's it. First year done. We mark the occasion with lunch at the newly opened Pancake House in town, and compare notes over the last 12 months.

Clive thinks the time has gone very quickly, that giving up work was the best decision he ever made and that it's been an easy transition. This is good news, of course, because I'd hate to think he was miserable. However, I don't quite agree.

Yes, I think it was a good decision. Work was making him miserable and, although we've missed his salary, his canny bookkeeping skills mean we are bobbing along nicely. However, the time hasn't flown by for me. In fact, some of the days have been the slowest I can recall. Nor has the change been without its challenges, though we have worked through the difficulties, which I freely admit have been largely down to my overwhelming desire to be in charge of everything all the time.

My main observation is that Clive has, to use the awful phrase, been on a journey, and he's definitely a happier, if tubbier, man than he was. He's rediscovered things about himself and learned new ones. He has opened himself up to new experiences and made new friends, rediscovered his connection with the earth and, I'm pleased to say, not yet invested in a model railway.

## POSTSCRIPT

There won't be a second volume of this diary, but it's perhaps worth mentioning that just days after I finished writing, Clive sliced through his leg with a Stanley knife, necessitating 13 stitches in his thigh; and he came through the casement window on to the balcony of our holiday flat with such graceless determination that I laughed so much I couldn't breathe.

Oh, and that archaeological dig was amazing and, amongst other things, Clive dug up the skeleton of a six-foot Roman.